Praise for Lillian Daniel and
When "Spiritual but Not Religious"
Is Not Enough

"This is the wonderful, essential Lillian Daniel at her best—earthy, perceptive, devout, tough-minded, angry, and laugh-out-loud funny, all in one. Daniel's easygoing style is just right for revealing her great gift of finding God in the everyday. Sometimes she is biting. Sometimes she is tender, and often what she says is stunningly beautiful."
—Bob Abernethy, executive editor, *Religion & Ethics Newsweekly*, PBS

"Here is why I love Lillian Daniel's writing: It is honest, it is funny, and it teaches me about Mary and Martha via a yoga class. Also, Lillian Daniel describes the church I know and am known by—she describes a church that is ordinary and extraordinary, full of people who are broken, gifted, blessed, strange, and wonderful. The church she describes is the place that has sustained my spiritual life when my own interior sense of God's presence has faltered; and it is the place that, as often as not, is where I am sitting when my sense of God's presence reignites."
—Lauren F. Winner, author of *Girl Meets God*
 and *Still: Notes on a Mid-Faith Crisis*

"You read some things because you have to or need to or ought to. You'll read Lillian Daniel for the pure pleasure of pitch-perfect writing—she has the rare talent of a 'natural.' Along the way, you'll discover enrichment and insight that you needed and wanted...Lillian cooks up a delicious and nourishing feast for readers. Don't miss it!"
—Brian McLaren, author of *Why Did Jesus, Moses, the Buddha, and Mohammed Cross the Road?* (brianmclaren.net)

"There are plenty of books that critique religion. But here's a good critique of the critics. Lillian is as fed up with bad religion as anyone else, but she's also careful to celebrate good religion and good spirituality that bring people to life and make the world a better place. She reminds us that God is always doing a new thing, but that doesn't negate the old things God has done over the centuries. Lillian reminds me of the old adage: 'The Church is a whore, but she's my mother.' May her book invite us to stop complaining about the Church we've experienced and work on becoming the Church we dream of."
—Shane Claiborne, author and activist
   (facebook.com/ShaneClaiborne)

"Lillian Daniel has a unique voice, a singularly charming mix of sweet and acerbic. She is often hilarious and always wise. This is one of those rare books that, when you finish the last page, you immediately want to start again at the beginning."
—Martin Copenhaver, senior pastor, Wellesley
   Congregational Church (United Church of Christ)
   and author of *To Begin at the Beginning*

"These days, when a good word for 'religion' is seldom heard, Lillian sings a joyful song to faith embodied in the gritty, funny, weird everydayness of the church. Somehow she manages to be both realistic and encouraging about that which the world facilely dismisses as 'institutional religion.' Lillian has given us one of the great books on life together in the congregation."
—Will Willimon, bishop of the United Methodist Church and professor of Christian ministry, Duke Divinity School

"Jews affirm that God is everywhere and in all of us, and Lillian Daniel makes that real in this delightful manifestation of the God within her that enables her to open our eyes more deeply to the wonder and miracles that are present in everyday life situations."
—Rabbi Michael Lerner, editor, *Tikkun Magazine*, and chair, the Interfaith Network of Spiritual Progressives

"With sly wit and insight Lillian Daniel provides powerful postmodern observations of spirituality, faith, and religiosity in America with wonderful ironic prose and a preacher's ear for language. Any person interested in the future of faith communities would do well to purchase this publication."
—Otis Moss III, senior pastor, Trinity United Church of Christ

When "Spiritual but Not Religious" Is Not Enough

Seeing God in Surprising Places, Even the Church

LILLIAN DANIEL

JERICHO
BOOKS ™

New York Boston Nashville

Jericho Books
Hachette Book Group
237 Park Avenue
New York, NY 10017
www.jerichobooks.com

Printed in the United States of America

RRD-C

First Edition: January 2013

10 9 8 7 6 5 4 3 2 1

Jericho Books is a division of Hachette Book Group, Inc.
The Jericho Books name and logo are trademarks of Hachette Book Group, Inc.

The Hachette Speakers Bureau provides a wide range of authors for speaking events. To find out more, go to www.hachettespeakersbureau.com or call (866) 376-6591.

The publisher is not responsible for websites (or their content) that are not owned by the publisher.

Library of Congress Control Number: 2012942095

ISBN 978-1-4555-2308-5

Contents

Part I
SEARCHING AND PRAYING

Chapter 1

Spiritual but Not Religious?

A MAN RECENTLY TOLD ME something about his faith life, as people are wont to do with ministers. He said, "I'm spiritual but not religious, and I want to give you my testimony, if you will, about why I do not attend church."

Now, can I just vent for a minute? When I meet a teacher, I don't feel the need to tell him that I always hated math. When I meet a chef, I don't need to tell her that I can't cook. When I meet a clown, I don't need tell him that I think clowns are all scary.

No, I keep that stuff to myself. But everybody loves to tell a minister what's wrong with the church, and it's usually some church that bears no relation to the one I am proud to serve. So I braced myself.

Like so many Americans, he had made many stops in the

new American religious marketplace, where we no longer have to stay in the tradition we were born in. Today, Americans shop for churches. I've moved from one church to another, and some of you probably have too.

So he was raised in the Catholic faith. He came to feel injured by that tradition, let down by it. His questions weren't answered or welcomed. The worship, the rituals, the preaching— it all felt pretty irrelevant.

So later, after college, he was drawn as a young adult into a conservative Baptist church. He had joined that church because of the great people, and even accepted Christ as his personal savior during a service. But later, after joining, he realized the church held all sorts of strict beliefs he could not contend with, the worst of which was a prohibition on dancing, not to mention a prohibition against sex before marriage, which as you know, often leads to dancing. What kind of God would not want me to use my body to move? He wondered, about that, and about the dancing. He drifted from that church.

Later, after marrying, he joined the church of his wife's upbringing, an open-minded liberal Protestant church in my own denomination, a church he described as a big warm hug. There, dancing and drinking were not frowned upon, and neither were his theological questions. In that intellectual environment, he was encouraged to use his mind to study the biblical narrative, to consider the history of the day and think critically about scripture. His questions, even his doubts, did not shock anybody, and in fact he was told all those questions actually made him a very good mainline Protestant.

But the marriage ended, and now that church really felt like his wife's, so he found himself spending his Sunday mornings sleeping in, reading *The New York Times*, or putting on his running shoes and taking off through the woods. This was his religion today, he explained. "I worship nature. I see myself in the trees and in the butterflies. I am one with the great outdoors. I find God there. And I realized that I am deeply spiritual but no longer religious."

He dumped the news in my lap as if it were a controversial hot potato, something that would shock a mild-mannered minister never before exposed to ideas so brave and different and daring. But of course, to me, none of this was different in the least.

This kind and well-meaning Sunday jogger fits right into mainstream American culture. He is perhaps by now in the majority—all those people who have stepped away from the church in favor of ...what? Running, newspaper reading, Sunday yoga, or whatever they put together to construct a more convenient religion of their own making.

I was not shocked or upset by the man's story. Naturally, I have heard it a million times before, so often that I almost thought I could improvise the plotline along with him. Let me guess, you read *The New York Times* every Sunday, cover to cover, and you get more out of it than the sermon. Let me guess, you exercise and where do you find God? Nature. And the trees, it's always the trees during a long hike, a long run, a walk on the beach. And don't forget the sunset. These people always want to tell you that God is in the sunset.

Like people who attend church wouldn't know that. Like we are these monkish people who never heard all those Old Testament psalms that praise God in the beauty of natural creation, like we never leave the church building. God in nature? Really? It's all over the Bible that we hear every Sunday, but these folks always seem to think they invented it.

But push a little harder, on this self-developed religion, and you don't get much, at least much of depth. So you find God in the sunset? Great, so do I. But how about in the face of cancer? Cancer is nature too. Do you worship that as well?

You see God in the face of your children, when they are saying loving things, or looking just like their grandmother, or saying something cute and winning about God.

Have you ever noticed that these spiritual but not religious adults, so averse to hearing about God in church, where adults have actually spent some time thinking about these things, never tire of hearing about it from their own children? These are the people who keep the "cute things kids say about God" chain e-mails in business.

"Let me tell you what my kid said the other day: 'Mommy, I think God is like the rainbow.'"

"Can you believe the wisdom of that?" says the proud spiritual but not religious parent.

Have you ever noticed that these people's children are always theological geniuses? They amaze their parents with their wisdom. What are the odds? I presume it is because, like most children, they are parroting back their parents' values. So the children also see God in nature but, because they are children and have bigger eyes, large heads, and high voices, they generally do so in much cuter ways. "I think there will be doggies and birdies and candy in heaven." Awww...

But let's take that a little further, junior. Will there be sharks and snakes in heaven too? Ewww. How about bloodsucking vampire bats? Now that'll keep you up at night, junior theologian.

These kids, teaching their parents with homespun aphorisms, are actually being poorly served. If they went to Sunday school they could ask about bats and scorpions in heaven. They could ask about cancer when a grandparent gets sick. They would have a place, a spiritual community, in which to go deeper.

But their parents, so afraid that the church is a place where they force you to accept their answers, have set up a vacuum in which the answers get invented without any formation or guidance. So when there are rainbows and happy kids it all works, but it's not so successful in the face of temper tantrums, selfishness, and dare I say it, sin. Because most self-developed Sunday morning ritual has little room for sin.

Or for disaster, for that matter. Suffering is seldom accounted for in these self-made spiritualities, other than as something we might overcome, by hard work, exercise, and reading the op-ed page. But worldwide disaster, how do you wrestle with that?

Well, here's how the man I told you about did it. Realizing that as a pastor I was desperately in need of reeducation, he went on to explain that his own little junior theologian, now a teenager, had bowled him over with another great insight, a brilliant thought exchange between father and son that made the dad realize his choice not to attend church was the right one, for his son had truly embraced the values he had always hoped he would.

Listen to what my son wrote, he said. "Children are starving with empty bellies in faraway lands. They have nothing to eat. All around them they hear the sounds of gunfire and bombs going off. And it made me realize that we are so lucky. We are so lucky to be living here and not there."

"I had tears in my eyes when he said that," the proud parent explained. "I was blown away and I realized, he gets it, he really gets it. It was gratitude. That's our religion—gratitude. And at that moment, when he recognized all that suffering and how fortunate he was, I could not have been prouder."

Never been prouder? I thought. Really? I mean, I can see being proud that your kid watches the news. I can see being a little proud that he understands himself to have privileges in this country that other people do not. I can see being a little relieved that he knows not everyone goes to bed with a full stomach, that he can at least imagine the fact that war causes unimaginable pain. But then what? The punch line from the religion of gratitude: "We're so lucky that we live here instead of there." Really? That's it? Never been prouder?

What's missing from that worldview—and this is no fault of the teenager—but what is missing from that worldview is the perspective that you might get in a Christian community that would take you from lucky to actually doing something about it. But this kid didn't get there. Or if he did get there, his dad didn't care enough to make it part of the story.

His dad was happy to stop with the self-made religion of gratitude, like a person who fills up on the deep-fried appetizers and doesn't order anything else from the menu. He may not feel hungry for dinner now, but that snack will not sustain him for anything like real exertion. It tastes good, but it's just not enough.

I am guessing that this family gives to charity and has a good supply of PBS tote bags. But when you witness pain and declare yourself lucky, you have fallen way short of what Jesus would do.

When you witness suffering and declare yourself to have achieved salvation in the religion of gratitude, you have fallen way short of what God would have you do, no matter what religion you are called to.

And by the way, while I think God does want us to feel gratitude, I do not think God particularly wants us to feel lucky. I think God wants us to witness pain and suffering and, rather than feeling lucky, God wants us to get angry and want to do something about it.

The civil rights movement didn't happen because people felt lucky. The hungry don't get fed, the homeless don't get sheltered, and the world doesn't change because people who are doing okay feel lucky. We need more.

As the scripture today tells us, "In accordance with his promise, we wait for new heavens and a new earth, where righteousness is at home." We can't sit back and simply feel gratitude, or feel lucky. No, as Christians we expect more, way more, like a new heaven and a new earth, and because we follow Jesus, we better expect to be involved in making it happen, alongside other people.

Gratitude is a biblically commended attitude. Feeling lucky is another religion altogether, one that says the gods pick one teenager to live in the suburbs of the richest nation on earth and another teenager to starve. In a worldview of luck, righteousness is really not at home.

But at some point the worldview of luck just doesn't pan out. At some point you realize that this isn't enough, and you long for something as outrageous as a new heaven and a new earth. At some point, if you think about it at all, that person with the self-made religion will use his God-given brain and the wisdom of hard experiences and start to ask angry and provocative questions about this spirituality of status quo.

"Who are you, God of sunsets and rainbows and bunnies and chain e-mails about sweet friends? Who are you, cheap God of self-satisfaction and isolation? Who are you, God of the beautiful and the physically fit? Who are you, God of the spiritual but not religious? Who are you, God of the lucky, chief priest of the religion of gratitude? Who are you, and are you even worth knowing? Who are you, God whom I invent? Is there, could there be, a more interesting God who invented me?"

I'm not against gratitude, any more than I am against finding God in a sunset or a child's eyes. Those are all good things, along with puppies, rainbows, great vacations, and birthdays. But here's the thing—none of that constitutes a religion, and I actually believe, contrary to popular wisdom, that in an age of spiritual people who are not religious, we need religion, and its dearest expression to this particular religious Christian person, the church.

I remember a family new to our church, whose grade-school-age kids had only a year of Sunday school under their belts. In the middle of what was his second Christmas pageant rehearsal ever, the little boy cried out in total exasperation, "Do you mean to tell me that we are doing exactly the same story we did last year?"

Today that youngster is grown up and has been blessed by the repetition that gives his chaotic days meaning. In a world that demands that everything be a one-time-only original production, the church remains a place to remember that there is someone much better than we are at original creations.

And let's get back to that proud father as an example. When he told me about his son, it finally hit me what was bothering me about this self-styled religion he had invented—he hadn't invented it at all. It was as boring and predictable as the rest of our self-centered consumer culture, and his very conceit, that this outlook was somehow original, daring, or edgy, was evidence of that very self-centeredness.

If we made a church for all these spiritual but not religious people, if we got them all together to talk about their beliefs and their incredibly unique personal religions, they might find out that most of America agrees with them. But they'll never find that out. Why? Because getting them all together would be way too much like church. And they are far too busy being original to discover that they are not.

But here in church, we hear scriptures like the one we heard today that tell us that originality and isolation are not the answer, where Jesus says to ordinary, fallible Peter, "Upon this rock I will build my church." In other words, you people are stuck with one another.

Now, let me acknowledge that on all sides of the Christian spectrum, there is much I do not want to be stuck with, from Koran-burning, pistol-packing pastors to the more ordinary preacher who was trying desperately to be inspiring and shouted out, "Let us launch into the depth of the sea, standing upon the rock that is Jesus!"

Really?

No wonder many good people get like the pop singer Prince—they want a new name for what they do, like the artist formerly known as Christian.

The church has done some embarrassing things in its day, and I personally do not want to be associated with a lot of it. But, news flash, human beings do a lot of embarrassing, inhumane, cruel, and ignorant things, and I don't want to be associated with them either. And here, I think we come to the crux of the problem that the spiritual but not religious people have with the church. If we could just kick out all the human beings, we might really be able to do this thing and meet their high standards.

If we could just kick out all the sinners, we might have a

shot at following Jesus. If we could just get rid of the Republicans, the Democrats could bring about the second coming and NPR would never need to run another pledge drive. If we could just kick out all the Democrats, the fiscally responsible would turn water into wine, and the church would never need another pledge drive.

But in the church, as everywhere, we are stuck with one another, and being stuck with one another, we don't get the space to come up with our own human-invented God. Because when you are stuck with one another, the last thing you would do is invent a God based on humanity. In church, in community, humanity is just way too close to look good.

It's as close as the guy singing out of tune right next to you in your pew, as close as the woman who doesn't have access to a shower and didn't bathe before worship, as close as the baby screaming, and as close as the mother who doesn't seem to realize it's driving everyone crazy. It's as close as that same mother who crawled out an inch from the heavy shell of postpartum depression to get herself here today and wonders if there is a place for her. It's as close as the woman sitting next to her, who grieves that she will never give birth to a child and eyes that baby with envy.

It's as close as the preacher who didn't prepare enough and as close as the listener who is so thirsty for a word, she leans forward for absolutely anything. It's as close as that teenager who walked here to church alone, seeking something more than gratitude, something more than newspapers and coffee, but instead finds a complicated worship service where everyone seems to know when to stand and when to sit and when to sing except for him, but even so gets caught up in the beauty of something bigger than his own invention.

Suddenly it hits that teenager. I don't need to invent God, because God has already invented me. I don't need to make all this up for myself. There's a community of folks who, over thousands of years, have followed a man who was not lucky, who, in the scheme of luck, was decidedly unlucky. But in the scheme of the church he was willing to die alongside the unlucky, to be raised from the dead, and to point out in that action that there is much more to life than you could possibly come up with. And as for the resurrection, try doing that for yourself.

Around that resurrection assumption, that humbling realization that there are in fact some things we simply cannot do for ourselves, raising the dead being the big one, around that humbling notion, communities of human beings have worked together and feuded together and just goofed up together, but we do it together because Jesus did it with these same types of people.

And thousands of years later, we're still trying to be the body of Christ; utterly human and realistic enough to know we need a savior who is divine.

At a historic Congregational church in New England, I had the pleasure of leading the church through a big anniversary celebration of the laying of the cornerstone of our third church building. This church had gone through some rough times, two church splits, some angry and painful departures of ministers, but things had been looking up and we were ready to celebrate.

We took two years gearing up for it, and in that last year all sorts of committees were at work, planning a special worship service, the choir rehearsing special anthems, guest speakers and half the church involved in cooking a feast, which, in the tradition of our Pilgrim forebears, would naturally be lasagna and garlic bread. It was going to be great.

And then just about a month before the big day, it came to our volunteer church historian's attention that there had been a mistake.

In calculating the date.

We had the wrong year.

Our building's seventy-fifth anniversary had been the year before.

There were hastily-called meetings, not official ones but those unofficial ones among the cognoscenti in the church where they pull one another aside in the bathroom to say, "Did you hear?," whispers at choir rehearsal and in the parking lot, those kind of meetings, serious debates among the long-term members as to whether or not we ought to even mention this mistake to anybody, or were we obligated to confess our error to the entire congregation?

But we were a small church and by the time you had asked enough people whether or not we should make public the news that we had missed our own anniversary, it was pretty much public already. In fact, I even had some other minister colleagues calling me up from other churches where the news had spread to say, "Really? Really? Your whole church missed its own anniversary?" In historic New England, that's pastoral misconduct.

By the time we arrived at the next church council meeting, everybody knew but no one had discussed it in any official way and the big anniversary Sunday was around the corner. Would there be blame, embarrassment, frustration, or forgiveness?

Finally in that reserved New England way, when we came to the regular agenda item that had for the last eighteen months been listed as "Anniversary activities," somebody said, without emotion, "And now we come to the small matter of the anniversary date of our church building, or perhaps we should say the actual anniversary date as opposed to the assumed date we have all been working with, and what should be done about said matter."

There was a long and awkward silence. And then finally someone said, "Well, I've done some research, and it turns out that it took them quite a while to complete the building after they laid the cornerstone. In fact, by the time the building was finished it was no longer the year they started, but it was a year later. So you see, it all depends on what this is the anniversary of. I mean, you can celebrate the anniversary of laying a cornerstone, but that's hardly fitting. Wouldn't it be more fitting to celebrate the anniversary of the completion of the building?"

Someone else chimed in, "Not the completion of the building, but the first worship service in it. That had to be that next year. I mean who celebrates the anniversary of a building? It's all about the people."

"Why, you're right, that makes so much sense. I can't believe we didn't see it this way from the very beginning."

To which a wise elder responded, "Ah, but I think we did."

So in a bit of revisionist history, and if you've ever served on a church committee, you know they are seed beds of revisionist history, our story changed from being a church that had wanted to celebrate the cornerstone of the building to a church that had always intended to celebrate the first worship service. And after some more whispered updates at choir rehearsals, in the bathroom, and around the parking lot, it was never mentioned again. This had always been our anniversary plan and it always would be.

I remembered the epistle: "Do not ignore this one fact, beloved, that with the Lord one day is like a thousand years, and a thousand years are like one day."

And so on every day, somewhere some tender, fallible, unlucky, lasagna-making, anniversary-forgetting community of faith celebrates an anniversary.

I want to say thank you to all those people. Thank you for being faithful to one another, for welcoming the stranger, and for worshipping the God who invented you and not the other way around.

Chapter 2

The Stand-in Church

PETE WAS THE SEXTON at the first church I served, in charge of maintaining the physical plant of the church. Sextons, not Saint Peter, hold the all-important keys in church life, securing the building after twelve-step meetings, cleaning up before Sunday worship, making sure the boiler is ready and running. A rock-and-roller who had turned his life around, Pete the sexton had finally met the right wife, finally quit drinking, and finally started to think about one day quitting smoking.

With his ever-present dark jeans and T-shirts, salt-and-pepper beard, and rock-star-skinny build, people were always telling Pete that he looked like Eric Clapton. He still played the guitar with other men in that New England suburb, who parked minivans after work and descended into basements where tube amps and Stratocasters kept out the noise of the children's cartoons upstairs.

As sexton, Pete spent as much time visiting with the church members as he did fixing up the church, more comfortable sharing his philosophy of life than hammering in solitude, unless it was on that guitar. The beauty of working with Pete was that he might come over to my parsonage to fix a leaky pipe, but he'd end up being convinced to have just one cup of coffee, and then another, and then another. Soon you'd discover that three hours had gone by. While the sink was not yet fixed, you sure had learned a lot about Masonic conspiracy theories, the hazards of a bad acid trip, or why life in the Connecticut suburbs had never been for Pete.

After I left that church, Pete and I remained friends as I followed the gossip of the church I had left behind over yet more cups of coffee, now in my own home, where leaky pipes did not beckon to him to be fixed. The news he brought from that old church was nuanced in that Pete did everything there except attend worship.

Scarred by church long ago, Pete had been drawn into an intellectual dance in which he read much about all religions but could not bear to rest in one. Fascinated and horrified by the life of faith, he had found a job that pulled him into the inner workings of a community of faith without demanding any confession of faith. In many ways, Pete practiced the Christian faith, but his early experience of a church obsessed with doctrines had left him gun-shy of the institution. While he never sat in those pews at the appointed hour, he was participating in the church in every other way.

When lung cancer caught up with him, when a cup of coffee became too heavy to hold, when bad cells had wrapped themselves around the last safe breathing space in his thinning body, his wife called me to a Catholic hospital, where I saw Pete be still for the first time in my life.

To watch his wiry, fidgety body at rest, moving only with the up and down of the respirator, to hear the gurgling of fluids in his chest that would end up bringing on a death by drowning, to watch the tears of the "right wife at last" as she held on to him in this small moment, I was suddenly the church.

A former associate minister, one who had stayed too short a time to affect much at all, I was suddenly the Church of Jesus Christ writ large, present at the moment when Pete would die, and I would witness my very first experience of life leaving one body and going somewhere else.

I think we do this for one another all the time, we mad people of faith. We interact with those who will not step foot in the institutions we love. We make friends with nonbelievers who claim that we are crazy. And then in these moments of utter crisis, we find ourselves called into the eye of the tornado. And suddenly we realize that we have become, for them, the church. And we are called to play a role greater than our role as friend, family member, or colleague.

"Do you believe in heaven?" they may ask, as Pete had asked me many times over coffee, just checking to make sure I still thought it was true.

"Do you still believe in God as you watch him suffer?" they may ask, as the wife of a dying man asked me, angrily challenging yet longing for some word of hope as her love slipped away. Forever?

And suddenly, instead of thinking that a debate is about to ensue, you realize you have been called upon not for your answer, not for your argument, but for your testimony. Not just your testimony, but the testimony of the church that has stood in the midst of utter sadness and made claims that only the mad would make.

Many quietly faithful people struggle with testimony. We don't want to shove our faith down people's throats. We don't want to be pushy, obnoxious, or self-righteous. But sometimes people put us on the spot, put us on the witness stand, and ask for our testimony.

Testimony is calling out that you have seen light in the midst of darkness. Testimony is telling the story about how you met God, even when you have forgotten it. Testimony is telling the story of a community over time, of a particular people, and how God has intervened. And when the unchurched call us into the most intimate and sad moments, we become the church. We can either sit mute or give our testimony.

It may not be eloquent. Some of the best testimonies are stumbling words choked out of the same sorrow that the nonbeliever stands drowning in, but at least the believer can say, "Yes, in the midst of this tragedy, I believe there is more than all of this."

I remember, when I walked into Pete's hospital room that day, that not only was my role unclear but my place was unclear. Was my role to be friend or to be some kind of pastor? What was my place in this situation?

And what was my place in this physical room? Pete's wife was next to him; there were no free chairs and no one to act as host. I wondered where to place myself.

Like the disciples who asked Jesus where they should sit, with regard to who could be at his right side, loved ones around the bed of a dying person often wonder the same thing. Where is my place?

There can even be a hierarchy of the grieving. Who sits closest? Who does the doctor address? Who is forgiven from speaking and who is called upon to explain?

And the newcomer, entering the room where death has settled, is always unsettled. Do I hold the hand of the one who is slipping away? Or do I hold the hand of the one who will be slipped away from?

In this case, I felt my place was at the foot of the bed. Pete's wife had his head in her arms, his heart next to her heart, but I at least could keep vigil over his feet. I rubbed his foot, first one then another, gradually realizing that indeed I had found my place, not just here but in a longer story.

The great prayers of the church, the testimony that life will go on and that the dead will live forevermore, often get heard from the feet up. They come, for most who grieve, as background noise in the surprising busyness of death. Even the details of the funeral overshadow the words that are spoken, and family members worry over who brought the chicken salad, or who will read the poem at the graveside.

But God has never objected to speaking from the bottom end of things. It was, after all, his son who washed the feet of the disciples who preferred to argue over who would sit at Jesus' right hand. Jesus preferred to proclaim from the foot of the bed, and to take his cues from the foot of his own body.

Sometimes, the church has to work through church stand-ins. Sometimes, as people of faith, we are called to witness the good news to people who have no interest in our beliefs. Yet they have called us to their sides at a moment of crisis, as friend, family member, or comforter. And we could no more leave behind our faith than we could leave behind our bodies. And so we are there, present, being as much of the church as they will see.

The membrane between the church and the world is thin. We want to cross it lightly, gracefully, so that suddenly, even for those who do not show up on Sundays at God's physical house, a house with many mansions still might shine through in their imaginations. This kind of agility is not born by taking the physical house, the church, lightly. No, worship is what prepares us for the strangeness of life. When we read about Jesus washing the disciples' feet before the Last Supper and his death, God prepares us for a later moment when the only seat at the table will be at the bottom of a hospital bed.

Rather than hammering the unchurched with the gospel from our mouths and heads, rather than arguing with them or badgering them, rather than capturing the moment like a pious pirate, the stand-in church is called not to be brilliant, not to be persuasive, not even to tell the entire story right then and there, but rather, the stand-in church is called to simply be.

After all, we follow a savior who knew when to preach but also when to be content washing feet. Jesus delivered the gospel from the bottom up. We can do that too. As I rubbed his feet, as the stand-in church, Pete's body buckled under the white blankets and left us with a violent shake of an old rocker whose guitar solo had taken it all out of him. I held on to his feet a little longer, as they grew cold, until I knew that this was no longer my place. It was time to move to the rest of the room and the tears of the living, where Pete's song played on.

Chapter 3

So Hard to Sit Still

YOGA CLASS ALWAYS BEGINS with meditation. Never mind that I have come there to get some exercise. Yoga teachers aren't like service providers who give you what you want when you want it. They don't just jump into things, like those hard poses you see in the pictures of really skinny people twisted up like pretzels.

I admire what they can make their bodies do—arching over like an upside down V in downward dog, with their feet flat on the floor, doing headstands without leaning against the wall, legs tucked behind their heads, or sitting with those same legs folded up in the lotus position. And here's the amazing thing: they always look comfortable, not pained, with no sign of agony or even a little discomfort.

Well, that's where my mind goes when I come to yoga

class. That's what I strive for. Even though I am at a basic level, I want to be like those people. So I go to class to challenge myself to get to the next level, really wanting to improve and do more than I did the last time, to look like the people in the pictures. When it comes to yoga, I want to achieve that kind of sainthood, but that's not the right word for an eastern practice. I want to achieve pretzelhood.

Which is, of course, not at all what yoga is about. I am reminded of that at the beginning of every yoga class, during what is always a painful and difficult time for me. Why is it painful? Is the first pose a hard one? Or an exhausting one? No, this is the beginning of class when we haven't done a thing and won't for a while. That's what makes it painful. We have to spend all this time at the beginning of class doing nothing and sitting still.

"Let's begin with some breathing," the yoga instructor explains, and inside I groan. "No, please, no breathing, let's just get on with it."

I'm wanting that great feeling you get, that physical release that comes from the physical practice, that same sense of well being that has entirely eliminated backaches from my life. I want that post-yoga stretched-out, blissed-out feeling that allows me to take everything else in the rest of my day in stride, and I want all that to start sooner rather than later.

"Ujjayi breathing, bouncing the breath off the top of the throat. Six counts inhaling, six counts holding, six counts exhaling."

Are you kidding me? What fresh hell is this? It's going to

go on forever; first six counts, then eight counts, then one nostril, then the other, and then back to something else boring. It's just breathing, for crying out loud. We can do this already.

Sometimes it's all I can do not to shout out, "Excuse me, but I came here to get some exercise. Can we just hit fast-forward on this part?"

But I look around and everyone else in the class seems to be really into it. They are relaxed as if this is the most natural thing in the world to be doing. Six counts through one nostril, six counts through the other. Don't these people, sitting there so calmly with their eyes closed, have anything to do?

My eyes are actually open, but furtively, secretly so. You see, I need to open my eyes periodically in order to check on the rest of the class, and make sure that their eyes are all shut. I also need to monitor the teacher to make sure her eyes are closed too. This is my job, you see, to check out what other people in the class are doing.

And to check the clock. That's my other job. I need to see exactly how much time we are wasting on meditation so that I can know exactly how frustrated to be.

Nobody in yoga class gave me these two jobs. I have graciously taken them on myself, since no one else seems to be taking that kind of initiative. They are too busy sitting still, breathing, and meditating.

At the risk of stating the obvious, yoga does not come naturally to me. I have nothing against the spiritual side of things. I just can't deal with it when it involves sitting still.

Which is why I really struggle with the story of Mary and Martha. It is all about Jesus praising someone for sitting still, a woman named Mary, who sat quietly in his divine, spiritual presence. Mary would be awesome with those first few minutes of yoga class.

But picture the scene. There Martha was, running around the house, getting food on the table for all the disciples. The entertaining pressure was on. This food was for Jesus for crying out loud. And Martha's making it all happen, because somebody has to.

In order for some people to sit around being still and having deep thoughts, I guarantee you there's always another group of people running around behind the scenes making it all possible, making sure the space is ready, the food is cooking, the music is prepared, and the atmosphere is just right for the other folks to have this deep spiritual connection in the moment.

Take church, for example. We sit in our pews, having the time to pray, to listen to the Gospel being read, and to connect with the divine in this beautiful, transcendent, holy space.

But out in the lobby, we've got a crew of people setting up coffee. They're listening to the sermon on the sound system speakers while they put out the cream, the sugar, and the cups. In my traditional Gothic brick church, they can actually watch the worship service while it happens on a TV monitor in the lobby while they work. Those coffee makers are no less spiritual. They're just highly caffeinated. And they want the rest of us to join them. They've found a way to go to church without having to sit still. If I were not a preacher, I'd be out there multitasking with them.

Downstairs and upstairs and in the nursery, there are folks watching and instructing our children so that the parents can take this moment of silence and peace. So right in the middle of a worshipping spiritual community, it takes a lot of busy people behind the scenes to create a space for other folks to sit still.

If you had been there with Jesus that day, who would you have been? Mary, sitting still, or Martha, making it all possible?

If I had been there that day, I would have been Martha, running around. I don't know if I would have been cooking or doing dishes, but I would have been doing something because, to be honest, that's just more comfortable for me. I don't like to sit still. Never have. Never will. And that's not easy in my field, where ministers are sort of expected to be meditative.

The truth is, most ministers are a lot better at sitting still than I am. I know this because when I attend clergy meetings, I feel like I'm in a high-security prison lockdown, where no one can leave and I'm the only one who objects.

When I represented our denomination as a delegate at our national church gathering, General Synod, we had to sit at these huge tables in a cavernous convention center, day after day, hearing speeches, watching worship, voting on things, for hours and hours at a time.

I got in trouble with our leader because she never saw me

sitting behind my nameplate in my spot, and she thought I was playing hooky. But I was there. I was just walking in circles around the perimeter of the convention center because I could not sit still. "How can you concentrate?" she asked, as though I were a misbehaving child in grade school.

"It's the only way I can concentrate," I replied. "I don't sit still. I need a lot of stuff coming at me." But I could tell she was not impressed. It was clear that she thought I was immature and I was somehow less spiritual because of it.

When did sitting still get equated with spiritual depth? Probably back in your youngest memories of sitting in an uncomfortable church pew, getting bribed with Life Savers and gum, while your mother said over and over again, "Just sit still," with such urgency that you could almost see Satan waiting with a big net to catch all those wiggle worms.

As if heaven will be full of people meditating in the lotus position, or sitting for long hours in eternal church meetings. If any of that is true about heaven, I at least want to check out what my options would be downstairs.

The truth is, many great religious heroes were people of action, doers of the word and not just hearers. In our church, for a very noisy week each summer, the junior high mission campers are running in and out of the church offices in between their projects, working on people's yards in the hot sun, feeding children across the world, weeding at the nature center. These kids work hard, and they bring an incredible energy into the building all week. Those weeks remind me that the Spirit is alive and God's work is getting done.

So on behalf of all the undercherished hyperactive people of the world, let's put away for good that old simplistic interpretation of the Mary and Martha stoiy that goes like this: Martha was more interested in doing housework than in listening to Jesus.

Give me a break. Of course Martha was interested in what Jesus was saying. After all, she had invited him to her house. This was a big deal for her.

I feel like I know Martha, and she absolutely would have been following Jesus' conversation, keeping track of it, as she went around doing this thing and that. Martha's not shallow, but like most women—and many men—she's a multitasker.

And as an excellent multitasker, Martha probably would have found Mary more than a little annoying, sitting there all goo-goo-eyed at Jesus' feet, Little Miss Meditative Mary, who can't walk and chew gum at the same time, listening as if the world depended on her hearing every little thing he was saying.

Martha would be used to the disciples acting that way, so devoted and spiritual and interested in every word from Jesus, while someone else brought them food and drink. Yes, she was used to the guys acting that way, the men just assuming that someone would wait on them. But Mary? Come on, Mary, not you too? Get over here and give me a hand. We can listen to Jesus while we work.

To which Jesus would have said, "Martha, Martha, you are distracted by many things."

Distracted? Here's what I would have said, if Jesus had

talked to me like that: "Don't call me distracted. I'm the only one with any focus here. I'm making this party possible. Everyone but me has just been sitting around, just being, just listening to you talk for hours. Can't we go *do* something? Jesus, isn't it time for your next healing miracle, your next lecture on world peace, and your next harangue against the religious establishment? I mean, please, can't we just get on with changing the world already? How dare *you* call *me* distracted!"

But Jesus did call her distracted, and it's preserved in scripture for us to read about two thousand years later.

So what was Martha distracted by? Along with her own work ethic, perhaps Martha was distracted by something bigger and more complicated, something so much a part of life and the air she breathed that she just couldn't see it. Perhaps Martha was distracted by gender, and gender roles, because they play an important role in this story, when you look at the historical context.

You see, by sitting at Jesus' feet and listening, Mary was breaking a gender rule of the culture. Women weren't supposed to sit at the feet of gurus. Women were supposed to be serving the food. Men got to sit and have deep thoughts, but not women. It wasn't their place.

So maybe Martha was distracted, upset even, by her sister's breaking of the social code. It wasn't just that she needed her sister's help in serving all these men their food, but she was confused, maybe even threatened, by her sister's behavior.

Mary was acting like a man, taking on a male privilege that

32

society did not, and would not, give her. And not only that, Jesus was commending her for it.

Taking it even further, Jesus made it clear to all the men and the women that day that women could be disciples too, saying, "Mary has chosen the better part, which will not be taken away from her."

Not by you, Martha, not by you, my male disciples, not by you, this society that says women can do only one kind of work, and not by the religions that tell you only men can be spiritual leaders. It will not be taken away from her.

It was like Jesus was saying, "Mary, your place in society may be exhausting and confining, but your place in God's realm is open and restorative. Martha and Mary, there is room for you both, but in this moment, Mary has chosen the better part, because it's brave and it's countercultural and it's daring. Don't hold her back, Martha. Don't put her down or make her feel small for doing this. In sitting at my feet, by taking herself seriously as a spiritual student, Mary is going for it. And Martha, Martha, don't you yank your sister down."

After the three minutes of meditation time at the beginning of yoga have passed, after what felt like three hours, I know from experience that it will only get worse before it gets better. Because now the teacher has started talking about things that make no sense.

"Now imagine your third chakra is opening up, to the color blue. While the air you inhale from your right nostril is the color red, and it makes bolts of lightning spray out in every direction. More advanced students, picture these bolts coming out of your third eye like a hose, or a snake whose subtle energy fans out like feathers from a bird's wing, because in yoga you can never have enough metaphors. Newer students, who are not familiar with the chakras and their meanings, just picture a unicorn dreaming of world peace."

Yoga teachers say all this in that special yoga voice, very soft and quiet and gentle, all the while telling you to do things that are absolutely insane. It's like a form of yoga voice hypnotism that then leads you right from strange breathing and meditation into bizarre physical adventures that they make sound quite normal.

"After you have held your ujjayi breath for eight counts, slowly lift your right leg and flex and point, and flex and point, then wrap that right leg around your neck. More advanced students, wrap it around twice, keeping your breath regular...while singing the Indian national anthem... silently, in only the right side of your brain. For a deeper challenge, inhale through your right nostril, and move into a handstand position. More advanced students, once you are in the handstand, don't use your hands. Just float, upside down, breathing, breathing, breathing."

Every spiritual tradition has some tension between action and meditation. Some tension between doing God's will and listening for God's will. Some tension between life here on earth and the interior life of the spirit. Some tension between acting and being.

In a yoga class, it's all pretty obvious. You begin with

breathing and meditation. Then you enter into physical practice, which can be exhausting or exhilarating. And then finally at the end, you always come back again to the meditation, all this taking place within an hour and a half.

You end as you began, by listening to your breath, feeling things in the moment. But the truth is, you are not at the same place as when you began. The back and forth of the hour has changed you and the meditation at the end is for me always quite different from the meditation at the beginning.

By the end, I have relinquished my two jobs of scrutinizing my classmates and watching the clock. Having spent time being active, I find myself suddenly more able to just be, suddenly able to be very still.

It is at the end of yoga class that we bow and say to one another "Namaste." That greeting gets translated into English in many ways, but the one I like is this: "The divine in me acknowledges the divine in you." I don't think we're able to see one another in that way before class. We have to get there.

They call the final pose in yoga shavasana, which means "corpse pose." You literally lie there like a dead person, your body totally relaxed, for as long a time as the teacher sees fit. Often the teacher will say, "For some people, this is the hardest pose in yoga." Because it is hard in our culture to justify being still. And it was hard in Jesus' day as well.

What I can overlook in the Mary and Martha story, what I can get distracted by, just like Martha did, is my own impatience and defensiveness. When I hear that story, I immediately want to defend being busy. And when I do that, I imply that these two states are polar opposites with no relationship to each other, when actually, that is just not true.

Acting and being are not opposites, but partners. Mary and Martha are not two different people, one getting it right and one getting it wrong. Mary and Martha are two halves of the human spirit, two parts that complement each other.

Mary and Martha aren't fighting out there. They are fighting in here, inside each one of us.

Do you ever feel it? Mary and Martha, wrestling within you?

When I ask someone how they are, I can almost predict the annoying answer. "Busy, I am so busy." It pains me to hear people who live good lives complain about being busy, especially when it's my own voice doing it. When I feel busy, I try to look for a better phrase, and the one that works for me is "rich and full."

I use it so much that the phrase has caught on around our church. "How are you?"

"I'm really busy... I mean, oops, my life is rich and full."

But could we have lives that are not only rich and full but also occasionally still and strong? Still and strong. It's an option.

Mary, in her stillness, wasn't being passive. She was being strong. By sitting at Jesus' feet, she was actually standing up to the men in the room who thought she had no place there. In doing nothing, she was actually doing something really important. In sitting still to listen to Jesus, she was actually saying, "I matter, I count, I am somebody." She was still but she was strong.

If Mary and Martha live inside all of us, who wins the wrestling match? Only you know the answer to that question. Nobody can answer it for you.

Have you set up your life so that it can be a fair fight, or is the contest rigged to mostly go one way? Only you know.

But I do know one thing. In order to even ask the question today, we need to slow down and be still, like we can be in church, or in yoga class, or wherever you can be like Mary and get quiet in a holy place.

But as a pastor, I do know one more thing. The holy places wouldn't be here if we didn't actively engage, like Martha, and do the hard work.

Do we have to choose? Or can we embrace both?

Rich and full. Still and strong.

Martha. Mary.

Amen. Namaste.

Chapter 4

An Honest Prayer

A NEW SEMINARY INTERN was offering the pastoral prayers one Sunday and received a request to pray for a woman who had a last name he found very difficult to pronounce. It was a name from a country whose language, Polish, most of us did not speak, and it sounded nothing like it was spelled. But in the intimacy of congregational life, we had learned how to pronounce it over the years.

So it was particularly painful to listen to the young man as he prayed out loud and kept stumbling over the name as he tried to get it right. He would make one attempt to say it, stop himself, try to say it another time, then stop again, wincing, and then butcher the name all over again. It was like it would never end.

Finally he let out an exasperated sigh that the whole congregation was relieved to hear, since it meant he would finally stop. Continuing with the prayer, he looked up to the heavens and said, "Oh God, you know what the woman's name is!"

It was an honest prayer. And the honesty was not just in his frustrated comment, but in his sigh to the heavens as well. He was being honest in his emotions in the middle of a prayer, and trusting that God could take care of the details.

Sometimes we pray to God with so much specificity, it sounds like we are lecturing a sloppy subordinate at work about when and where to show up for the key event, complete with last names, details about the hospital room number, and the exact diagnosis, when what God really desires is an honest emotion, straight from the heart.

I have always wanted to have a cottage by a lake. But when a friend suggested I pray for it, I recoiled. "First I should pray for health," I said. "And not just my own, but my family's."

"Don't forget world peace," he added. "And a cure for all diseases. Be sure to name them all, with their appropriate Latin names, so God knows exactly what your instructions are, because we wouldn't want hangnails to be eliminated before cancer. But yes, there's a lot to cover before you can ask for a cottage."

That kind of thinking, that reluctance to ask God for what we really want, is arrogance posing as humility. It seems humble to not ask God for our own desires, and to put other larger matters first. But doing that seems to imply we have power in all this. As if by asking God to cure diabetes before asking for a raise, we might actually affect God's priorities.

Do we honestly think that if no one asked for anything trivial, and everyone got focused on world peace, God would finally see that we had reached some quota and say, "Right, now that four billion and one people have asked for it, I will make it happen. But don't anybody ask for a cottage by a lake right now, or I'll get distracted."

Sorry, but I just don't think our prayer requests have that kind of power. So why pray then?

Prayer is about connecting with God, about having a relationship with our divine creator. God desires that with us, and because God loves us so much, God actually cares about our trivial wants, our big dreams, and our petty grievances. This is humbling news indeed. We can come to God with anything, and God will work with it.

When I do have a selfish desire, prayer inevitably helps in that it exposes it. By praying for what I really want, I am sometimes shamed into realizing I should not want that thing after all. When you are actually praying something like, "Please don't let him get that job because if that pompous moron has any more success in life, it will drive me so crazy with jealousy I won't be able to sleep..." you can't help but notice that this is not the person you want to be.

When you just think these things, your mind allows the toxicity to bubble along, unchecked, but when you lay a desire like that out in front of God, it gets exposed. And once exposed in prayer, God can work on it with you. And a prayer for another person's downfall might be transformed into a prayer that envy would lose its sin-soaked hold on your heart. But you can't get there without first passing go, without first asking for a pony, a cottage, your friend's job, or even her husband. God wants to hear our honest prayers.

Prayer is full of surprises for me. When I begin, I think I am praying for one thing, but by the end of the prayer, I have amazed myself at what I have come up with. I didn't know I was so worried about a family member, until her face dominates my mind during prayer time and shuts out the very thing I thought I had wanted to pray for. That prompts me to make a phone call after my "amen," which in turn leads to more adventures.

Sometimes, when I am praying for something I know is foolish, I come to the realization that there is a deeper need beneath it. Praying for an extravagant vacation to Hawaii might really be a prayer to spend more time with family, to be somewhere where the computer and the cell phone do not reign supreme. Before the "amen," God has revealed all kinds of ways I might connect more deeply with the people I love, and none of them require an airline ticket. By the end, I may still want the vacation, but in prayer, God has taken my desire and led me someplace new.

One of my favorite places of prayer is the Benedictine abbey at Saint John's University in rural Collegeville, Minnesota. You drive and drive through fields of soybeans and suddenly you see the college, marked by an architecturally stunning building that looks like a set piece from a futuristic science fiction movie, a massive structure of poured gray concrete that demands attention from the heavens, completed in 1960 and designed by the Hungarian architect and former member of the Bauhaus Marcel Breuer. Inside, the concrete swoops and allows light in through modern stained glass at odd angles, and the monks' seats in the choir are all geometric little compartments that separate one worshipper from another as if in astronauts' seats, each of us the pilot on our own little prayer adventure. During the regular times of prayer throughout the day, the monks are joined by the rest of us, students, artists in residence, a world-famous potter, and writers like me who come for workshops on the craft of spiritual writing, all in the setting where Kathleen Norris produced her beautiful book *Dakota: A Spiritual Geography*, which explores her Presbyterian roots in South Dakota, in conversation with artsy Benedictine monks in Minnesota.

Benedictine monks have a simple rule that states: "Let the brothers serve one another," written at a time when sisters might not have been on the radar screen. But at Saint John's they are known for their ecumenical vision to have artistic and literary conversations across the barriers that divide the church. They have produced an illuminated Bible, each page hand-painted in colors and in gold leaf, a project from medieval times but one that will be admired by Methodists and Muslims as it goes on its rock-star illuminated Bible international tour. No wonder so many people find it easy to pray in a place where the soil seems to be soaked in the art of the creator, a place that brings out the creativity of those who happen upon it in the fields, just a few miles away from the Cracker Barrels, the Menards, the Aldis, the T.G.I. Friday's, the McDonald's, and the ubiquitous Taco Bells. Just off the highway and through the cornfields lies a landscape of prayer.

But having just said that it is easy to pray there, it is not always. Leaving a session with the other writers, I was inattentive to their small talk, eager to walk out at exactly 11:45 a.m. to make the noontime worship, a ten-minute walk away. It would be one of five short services each day where scripture is read, songs that I don't know the tune of are sung, and we sit in our own little cubbies and soak in a tradition that is not any one tribe's to own. But I had yet to make it to one worship service that week, and now it was Wednesday. I had things and people to pray for, a ticket to punch.

But on the way there, I was joined by two other writers, and the walk slowed to a snail's pace and the conversation intensified, and by the time we entered, the monks and the laypeople in the choir loft were well under way. We slipped in the back, behind the organ, into three little seats with their individual bookshelves, one book for each service and for each person. The monks wore black shirts, the students wore sweatshirts, and the latecomers stumbled in wearing garments of shame, unaware of where we were in the service, straining to look over a monk's shoulder to see if he was on page 82 or 92. Okay, now I knew I had the right page, but I still wasn't saying the right words of the right psalm, and he was sitting down just as I was standing. Oh no, I was in the evening prayer book, and this was midday. Back to page 82—or was it 92? By the time I finally got my book open to the right page, the final song was sung and the monks were processing out, all leaving through a tiny door at the back of the abbey church, into the monastery, which was off-limits to the rest of us, who watched them, the majority of the small congregation, leave, and all the rest of us in our sweatshirts and clothes of many bright colors were left looking garish and mismatched after the sea of men in black had pulled back as if in a wave, leaving us like little mismatched seashells on the sand.

"That's it?" I said. "We missed it. I had no idea it would be over so soon."

"Don't blink or you'll miss it," said the Presbyterian I was sitting next to, as we extracted ourselves from our little monk pods. And the part of me that thinks that prayer is all up to me, that thinks that everything depends upon what I do and say, that part of me thought, "What a waste of time."

But then I considered the monks, who worshipped here in the same way not once a day but five times. Did they ever get bored or distracted and wonder if what they were doing made a difference? A friend had told me a story about a Minneapolis college professor who had brought his undergraduates out to the abbey to meet the monks. He had prepared them to meet a group of men who had chosen a life entirely apart, to be respectful of their different choices and of their meditative way of life. But when they finally sat down with a young novice in training, just a year or two older than the college kids, his

44

entire goal seemed to be to convince them the monks were no different at all. "We do all the things you guys do," he exclaimed animatedly. "We watch *American Idol*, we play video games! It's great here!"

The professor was disappointed. He had wanted his students to see a life apart, something exotic, but instead they just got to see life. Video games, black robes, *American Idol*, prayer five times a day, fraternity mixers, a trip to an abbey, a shared prayer service on a hot summer day. We're all just people, trying to get it right before God.

My thoughts went back to the seminarian who had botched the woman's name, mangling it so horribly her relatives had cringed, but I doubt that God cringed when he finally said, "Oh God, you know what the woman's name is."

And I thought, "Oh God, you know what time worship was supposed to start today." Yes, I had missed most of the prayer service, but I had not wasted my time. Any more than the monks who were there had wasted theirs. In prayer we have to lean in to one another, in to the generations that have gone before. Today and tomorrow the monks will pray in Collegeville and you and I will pray here, and together we will pray one another into an honest prayer that depends less on us than it does on God.

Oh God, you know. You already know it all. Amen.

Chapter 5

An Orphan Looks Ahead
to Father's Day

A T THE AGE OF FORTY-SIX, I feel a bit silly referring to myself as an orphan, but technically that's what I am. When I was thirty-three, I lost my mother, and my father died when I was thirty-nine. Not a day goes by when I do not think about and miss them both.

So occasions like Father's Day sneak up on me with echoes of grief. In the days ahead, I will find myself thinking, "I need to get a card and get it in the mail," only to remember that my father has been gone for years.

Back when he was alive, it was not uncommon for me to miss the deadline and send a belated card, days later. But now, I miss having someone to send that belated card to.

There's a Bible passage where Jesus says, "I will not leave you orphaned." People back then were no different from me.

We don't want to be orphaned, but most of us will outlive our parents.

I like the idea from the Old Testament that God is the father of the orphans and the protector of widows. This psalm means that someone is watching out for those of us who grieve. God's divine power is at work trying to give us what we are missing. If we need fathering, or mothering, or just plain loving, God is already on it.

For some people, Father's and Mother's Day are sad times not because they miss their parents, but because they do not. Not everyone gets the father they deserve in this life. That's why getting God matters even more.

Part II
CONFESSING

Chapter 6

We and They

SOME PEOPLE HAVE GRANDMOTHERS who teach them how to make waffles. Mine taught me how to make her a gin and tonic. That was the easy part. What was hard was getting the gin bottle out from inside the raw chicken, where it was hidden in the fridge.

My mother's mother, my grandmother from Anderson, South Carolina, was a card-carrying eccentric. She was almost the anti-grandma. In fact, we were not allowed to call her Grandma, Nana, or anything like that. Her fourteen grandchildren all called her Ms. Calhoun.

Ms. Calhoun was a brilliant woman, witty, with a devilish sense of humor and strong opinions. Seldom without a Pall Mall cigarette in her hand, she was stylish, a great fan of an outfit you seldom see anymore, the caftan. But her mood could turn at the drop of a hat.

One minute she might be making you fudge, a normal grandparenting activity. But then the next she'd have you making prank phone calls. At her initiative. To her friends. I remember saying, "Ms. Calhoun, I don't want to call any more of your friends and ask them if they have Prince Edward in the can. I'm tired of getting yelled at by people I hardly know for no good reason."

Already I was showing the markings of a pastoral leader.

On many an occasion Ms. Calhoun could be found standing out in her yard in a lace and silk bathrobe, firing a BB gun, allegedly at her neighbors' squirrels, but we all suspected she was firing at the neighbors themselves.

It may not surprise you to hear that this woman had somewhat strained relationships with those who lived next door to her. And it may also not surprise you to hear that she had no idea what they had against her.

She did, however, know what she had against them. They were unjust and unfair accusers.

What the neighbors said was that Ms. Calhoun's large dog, Amos, ran wild around the neighborhood late at night, knocking over everyone's garbage. They would awake to find a mess all over the sidewalks, grocery bags shredded and torn up, tuna fish cans thrown around, leftover food rotting on front doormats, all because Amos had been at work.

Now, every dog escapes and does this once in a while. Dog owners, maybe your dog has done it. But you probably felt guilty, tried to prevent it from happening too often, and felt remorse, even shame.

Ms. Calhoun, on the other hand, followed the defense policy of total deniability. Even when people had seen Amos at the scene of the crime, she would state without blinking an eye that her dog had been inside asleep by her side the entire night.

Finally, Amos died, after a long life of adventure and a steady diet of newspapers and plastic wrap. The small Southern neighborhood breathed a sigh of relief. Finally, there would be peace in the valley.

Yet, just two days after Amos's sad death, the neighbors awoke to find trash and garbage everywhere.

And then about a week later, the same thing happened again.

Clearly, this was not Amos. And the community, in their smug superiority, had been so quick to judge the eccentric woman with the odd habits, and in turn her eccentric dog.

But now, after his death, they had been proven wrong. It was as if, in pointing out the specks in her eye, they had missed the log in their own. The specks were her failings, but the log in their eyes was their snap judgment and criticism of another person.

In those weeks after Amos's death, when they cleaned up their garbage, they began to wander over to Ms. Calhoun's driveway and speak a few awkward words of apology. "We were just certain it was Amos," they said. "I mean, we saw him out there once or twice."

And years later, every time a critter knocked over the garbage, the neighbors would glance over toward my grandmother, who eyed them reproachfully from her lawn chair as they picked up the dirty diapers, bottles, and cans from their driveways.

That strange mutt Amos lived on in memory for years as a reminder that we should judge not, lest we be judged.

And then, a few years after his death, someone in our family actually spied the creature that was knocking over trash cans. It was not a runaway dog, not a sneaky raccoon, not a mischievous cat, but a much rarer species of scavenger heretofore unknown in the small Southern town. It was a Pall Mall–smoking, lace-bathrobe-wearing grandmother, sneaking out every few months at three in the morning to knock over her neighbors' trash cans and avenge the memory of Amos. Years after his death.

For she would not be judged. Even though she was wrong. She would make them wrong too.

What would the world look like if we were to all take Jesus' words from the Gospel to heart and stop judging one another but instead live together in generosity?

In this ridiculous story of a small Southern town, the cycle of judgment and defensiveness never ended, not even with the death of the perpetrating dog, who really was guilty of the crime he was accused of.

But if this story is so ridiculous, why do we fall into these traps and cycles in the church? How many of you hear people of faith rehash the past with as much variation as the different players in this story? And as much bitterness? And blaming?

These were people—and one hapless animal—who were so

caught in a cycle of blame and excuse-making that the original offense had ceased to matter.

And in that cycle, they had ceased to see one another as real people.

They were so caught up in winning the blame game, it wasn't fun anymore.

Well, okay, maybe my grandmother was having a little bit of fun.

But the log in her eye was enormous. And that had to cause some pain.

When Jesus says, "You hypocrite, first take the log out of your own eye, and then you will see clearly to take the speck out of your neighbor's eye," it's not just a scolding, it's a prescription for a better life, as in "You need to do this." As in, "We need to do this."

My grandmother never got that log out of her eye and her life in the neighborhood devolved into a small world of "me" versus "them." She sat perched on the lawn chair in her yard with a BB gun, distant from her neighbors. I look back and recall that I never knew any of her neighbors' names. They were always "them."

At the clergy gathering comes the inevitable "check-in" moment.

"Let's all go around the table, give your name, and your setting," says the host pastor, "and then share a little something about how your ministries are going."

Why do we do this? By now, don't we know how easily

these round tables may devolve into one of two extremes, the whining session or the bragging extravaganza? And yet we continue to throw clergy together in rooms and ask them to share. It's a disaster waiting to happen. We're only human. Our professional gatherings can go wrong in the same way everyone else's can.

The first comment often sets the tone. Who will speak first? A struggling pastor or someone who is enthusiastically succeeding? Either one can be dangerous.

The senior minister of the largest church represented speaks up. "I would really like to hear from any of you about how you deal with overenrollment in your youth programs." This comment elicits no response from the other pastors, who have shrinking youth groups. They look down at their coffee. "And recruiting top-notch staff... Where are the candidates?" The other pastors shift in their seats.

The pastor of the second biggest church pipes in sympathetically. "It's really tough to keep them too, even when you pay well." The small church pastor who wasn't depressed when he arrived is rapidly becoming depressed.

In the clergy group, if someone is brave enough to break the bragging streak, the conversation can head in the other direction to the woes and worries of the ministry. Granted, we clergy need a space to vent and unwind and sometimes a pastor's burden is so great, it spills out.

The clergy response to such a colleague can go one of two ways. On the side of angels, it can be a moment of empathy, when the brave soul who tells the truth realizes she is not alone. The pastor who worries that her church can only do confirmation every three years when once they had full classes every year hears that she is not the only one. The newly ordained minister learns that there are other clergy who cannot find enough hours in the day. The long-term pastor discovers that someone else in the room is also wondering when on earth to retire. The preacher learns that everyone is wondering what to preach this Sunday, after Monday's earthquake that has buried thousands of Chinese schoolchildren, and together they encourage one another to turn back to the Word one more time.

But a moment of weakness can occasionally become a pile-on, where negativity, fatalism, and blame take over the room like a toxic gas. When it goes wrong, each pastor comes up with a story worse than the one before, until the happy clergy start to believe that they must be in denial as to what is really going on. One story after another is told about congregations who make life difficult for their pastor.

I have found that when this happens, I listen less to *what* is said, and more to *how* it is said. And perhaps it's because I hail from a matriarch with a BB gun trained on "them," the key words, the ones that are most evocative, are "we" or "they," as in the congregation.

Does the pastor vent by saying, "We really have to amp up our pledging or we will be in trouble at budget time"? Or does she say, "These people have got to understand...I keep telling them...if they want more programs they need to give more..."?

"They." The telltale "they."

Often the language of "they" is mixed with the diagnostic language that has become popular in ministry circles. Sometimes the congregation is described as a patient or a dysfunctional organization. The use of the pronoun "they" implies that the doctor, consultant, expert, or fixer is none other than the pastor. "They" need fixing, and "I" am the one to come in, from the outside, and do it.

But Jesus once said, "Do not judge, so that you may not be judged." And then he adds, as if he had been addressing a group of clergy, "For with the judgment you make you will be judged, and the measure you give will be the measure you get."

In college and graduate school, we are taught the tools of critique. We're taught to aim and fire, to diagnose the problem or the weakness, to "shoot holes" in another person's argument. The more schooling you get, the more this is rewarded. The smartest one in the room is the distant critic, disdainful and separate.

I know that ministry can be hard, and that congregations can be frustrating, and that we ministers can also be frustrating to our congregations. Clergy need a place to relate to one another, to share their hopes, passions, and even their failures. But I worry at a particular tone some clergy take to the "they" who have called them as pastor. I worry about the damage that taking a critical distance can do. "They."

The image of the body of Christ flies in the face of such talk. Paul is clear that while the church body has many members, we are all still part of one body. In other words, we are a "we."

In recent decades the language of patient and doctor, or consulting organization and consultant, has swept the church, but I am ready for the pendulum to swing back. Certainly there are times when a consultant, or a denominational official, or an expert of some kind can come in and offer a fresh perspective, a legitimate analysis of the congregation as a "they." But when the pastor of six months or six years talks this way, I worry.

"I have been trying to explain to this congregation," he continues, "but I don't think they get it..."

And I think, "I don't think *you* get it." Until "they" becomes "we," there is no body of Christ. Just a would-be expert and a bunch of people who don't know "they" need to be fixed.

Pastors who refer to their churches as "we" are less likely to objectify and more likely to identify. They are less likely to see the speck in their neighbor's eye, as they are to see the collective speck that is troubling the whole body. Seeing that speck is where real ministry begins.

They are more likely, I believe, to move their congregations, not because the church thinks they are right, but because the church knows that we are loved.

These pastors are aware that as a "we," the most important member of the plurality is Jesus, who binds us together as the body of Christ, clergy and laity alike. So that nobody, even the pastor, gets to camp out alone in a lawn chair with a BB gun, cursing the neighbors.

No, we're called to be the church, to share the backyard and gather around the picnic table with garbage-chasing dogs, judging neighbors, finger-pointing experts, eccentric old ladies, somehow all of us invited by Christ to be a "we" in a world of "theys."

Chapter 7

Magic Tricks

RECENTLY I ATTENDED a clergy conference where this remarkably talented presenter from Cambridge University was not only lecturing brilliantly about theology and music, but would periodically sit down in the middle of his lecture at a grand piano and actually play the piece in question, completely from memory, with the skill of a Carnegie Hall star. On top of that, he had a cool British accent. Between the piano playing and the accent, it felt like he was cheating.

I was angry with God because I couldn't play the piano. (Like that's God's fault.) Of course, I was jealous of his gifts. Spare me this Anglican priest who's good at everything.

God is *so* not a communist when it comes to apportioning talent. And I think the progressive, liberal church needs to pass a resolution correcting God on that, because that's how we roll.

I was already feeling insecure that day because we had these Christian magicians coming to my church for a Wednesday night program that week. They're not only magicians but also ordained Methodist clergy. And I could just see my members saying, "Okay, Lillian, what special thing can you do, then?"

And I would have to say, "Look, I'm sorry, but there are just way more requirements to becoming a Methodist minister."

They pulled scarves out of boxes and hats, some with the American flag on them and finally one with the face of Jesus. They were careful to explain that this was not real magic, and certainly not black magic, but merely illusion.

Thanks for the heads-up, guys. Otherwise we all might have thought the Methodists were sorcerers, for sure.

You know the good thing about being stupid? It makes magic better.

Rachmaninoff-playing Anglicans, Bible-based Methodist magicians—it all just makes you feel inadequate. And when that happens, it's easy to get mocking and accusatory.

That's what happened with Jesus. Whenever he did good things in the world, whenever he was healing and teaching, the people accused him of doing magic tricks and working with the devil.

It's easy to be critical of other people's skills, but much harder to see the Holy Spirit at work in the gifts and talents of others. It's not easy to keep those demons of petty jealousy at bay.

But how remarkable that God can work through the piano-playing Anglican, the scarf-producing Methodists, and even through me.

I still wish I could play the piano though.

Chapter 8

Sing Sing

THE CLASS OF STUDENTS preparing for ministry sat around the table with their books open, ready to begin the three-hour seminar. They were all adults, mostly in their forties and fifties, one or two in their sixties. And unlike many seminary classes I come across, it was unusual in that there were no women. All the students were men.

Most of them were from the New York area, since that's where we were, but the class had an international flavor, with two students from China, one from Puerto Rico, and one from Medellin, Colombia.

They were, in some ways, an elite group. Fifteen of them had been chosen from among hundreds of applicants for this unique master's degree program in urban ministry. Some of them had applied year after year and been turned down, but now, this year, finally they were accepted.

There was a palpable energy in the room as their teacher introduced us that afternoon, for they had been reading a book I wrote with Martin Copenhaver, called *This Odd and Wondrous Calling: The Public and Private Lives of Two Ministers,* and my coauthor Martin and I were their guest speakers for the day.

Now, that book is all about the ministry, so it gets used in seminary classes, and students seem to like it fine, but in this classroom, their copies looked particularly well read and dog-eared, and their questions indicated that they had the intellectual chops for a rich theological discussion.

"What is the nature of authority in the church?" one student asked, and then the teacher asked them, "What are the signs of authority here?"

"Handcuffs, judges, and courtrooms," one man said. "Nightsticks, guns, uniforms..."

"And don't forget mace," said another.

"Yeah, mace," sighed one, squinting his eyes as others laughed. And it was then I remembered that I wasn't in Kansas anymore. This was not my usual teaching territory of a seminar room in an ivy-covered neo-Gothic building in Hyde Park, Chicago.

No, this class was in another historic building, one constructed at about the same time as many famous universities, but this one was not dedicated to the freedom of intellect. This one was dedicated to a lack of freedom, to the incarceration of violent criminals in Ossining, New York; hence its name: Sing Sing, a maximum-security prison out in the tony suburbs.

Sing Sing, a stately but dilapidated building surrounded by fences, barbed wire, and armed gateposts, sits right on New York's beautiful Hudson River. That's where the expression "sent up the river" came from, as did Sing Sing's nickname, "the big house." Because if it weren't for all the armed guards and fences, you might think it was a stately old mansion that had fallen into disrepair.

And, in fact, as the towns around it have become more posh and affluent, there has been a move by some residents to shut it down. It does not fit the image of successful yuppies commuting into New York from the suburbs. Why can't it be somewhere rural, out of view and out of mind?

But prison advocates want to keep it where it is, near enough to the city so that the prisoners can receive visits from their families and friends during long sentences in a maximum-security prison.

To teach this class we had to fill out all sorts of paperwork months in advance, and we finally got official approval from the governor's office to come. So with all that, it seemed strange that the way to get into the prison was to simply walk through the guard post and the parking lot and up to the front door, where we knocked and waited to see if they would let us in. We ended up standing at that front door for almost an hour as they tried to figure out if my Illinois driver's license with a renewal sticker on it was legitimate. And finally they cleared the prisoners who were mopping the floors out of the way and brought us inside the big house, where we signed our names in what appeared to be an ancient book, enormous and heavy with yellowed pages and signatures through the years. It was like the old pictures of God's giant book of life, but this one seemed also to have the aroma of death, or life stood still.

From there, we went through what seemed to be a thousand clanking doors that slammed locked behind us every hundred feet as we went farther and lower and deeper into what felt to me like some sort of catacomb or underground tomb.

Suddenly I realized that this was not the sort of place where you could turn around and say, "You know what, I think I left something in my car" or "Hey, I've changed my mind." I couldn't run back and scratch my name out of the book. I was now locked deep inside, downstairs in a basement classroom with a long table, bookshelves, and fifteen men sitting around it patiently waiting for us to be processed, for my driver's license to be accepted as real, for the stars to align. They seemed used to waiting, but when they saw us they jumped to attention, extending handshakes and making jokes, as though they knew we might be nervous.

While my graduate students that day were prisoners, when they did the usual classroom introductions it was just like any other class, but with one small difference. They gave their names, where they were from, and what they hoped to do with the degree one day, but then they all added, although they had not been asked to, how many years they had been inside.

Noticeably missing from the introductions was any mention of why they were there, but there are a limited number of violent crimes that land you in a maximum-security prison, and my imagination filled in the rest, which led to a moment of fear. What was I doing here? I shook, and then tried to pretend it was just a shrug. But I shook.

I found myself recalling Easter Sunday when the two Marys went to the tomb where, three days earlier, they had laid the body of their beloved friend and son Jesus but found the tomb empty. An angel of the Lord was waiting for them to explain that Jesus was missing not because someone had stolen his body, but because he had been raised from the dead, just as he had predicted. The guards were terrified, and the scripture reads that they shook and became like dead men.

They shook and became like dead men.

I have always thought that was such an interesting description of what fear does to you. You become like the dead, still living, but not really living.

Life delivers everybody frightening experiences; whether they are delivered on the schedule of a monthly bill or a daily newspaper, life delivers its share of fear.

There's no shame in being afraid. You just don't want to stay that way, to allow yourself to shake and become like the dead. Because the heart of the resurrection is that new life is always possible. Nobody should live in fear and be like the dead. God wants us to live like the living, not the dead. We're not meant to live like the dead. And we're not meant to treat other living people like the dead either.

But even though I believe that, it was my sin that took over my first thought when I was first invited to speak to a ministry class where the students were in prison for decades, or for life. My first thought was, "Why are they training for the ministry?"

If you're in prison for life or until you are an old man, what's the point of training for a career you may never get to practice?

And then it hit me, and I was so ashamed of my assumptions. I was assuming that ministry was something that happened in a church. But these men were preparing for a ministry that happened right where they lived, right there in prison, or perhaps back in the neighborhoods where they had committed their crimes. Their lives were not frozen while they were there; they were not like the dead, but among the living, trying to figure out God's call on their lives right there where they were.

That day at the tomb, the guards were frozen still, terrified, and like the dead. And the women may have been scared, but Mary and Mary stayed enough in the land of the living for the angel to talk to them. You see, when you check out in fear, you may miss God's message. But if you can hang in there and, no matter how bad the circumstances, if you can refuse to be like the dead and say, "No, in this moment, I am fully alive," then angels may whisper in your ear.

So it was to the women that the angel said, "He has been raised," and then, as if it was the most normal thing in the world, said, "He is in Galilee." Like, "You're looking for Jesus? Oh, I just saw him, he's in Galilee."

69

So apparently being raised didn't mean Jesus was still in heaven, but that he had been to heaven and was now walking around in a nearby village. The women had been given a chance to go meet Jesus and they took it, racing off to tell the others the good news.

And the good news is this, that no matter how trapped you feel, your freedom in Christ is more powerful. No matter how futureless you feel, your future in God is limitless. And no matter how big the dead end sign is at the end of the street, with Christ all things are possible.

Decades after the resurrection of Jesus, there was a man named Paul who had committed violent crimes against his fellow human beings. In fact, the very people he loved to beat and to torture were those Christians who preached a message of love that made him sick. He collected taxes for the empire, which meant that he brutalized poor people and skimmed off a profit for himself. He was a cruel and brutal man, and we know this about him because he admits it in the letters we read from him so often in church.

But then one day on the road to Damascus, this man was struck down and blinded for a moment by the Holy Spirit, and when he came to, he was a new man in Christ. The idea being that once Christ was raised from the dead, we all have the possibility to be raised and to live our lives differently than we would have otherwise.

So after his conversion, and once he had become the leader and founder of churches we still read about around the world two thousand years later, Paul wrote, "So if you have been raised with Christ, seek the things that are above, where Christ is, seated at the right hand of God."

Because Paul understood that while a person might undergo a personal transformation, your life situation around you doesn't change. So you still have the same life struggles, but you are now trying to be God focused. So his advice?

He said, "Set your minds on things that are above, not on things that are on earth, for you have died, and your life is hidden with Christ in God."

Sometimes you just have to do that: "Set your minds on things that are above, not on things that are on earth."

I came back from this trip to Sing Sing transformed. The conversation had been both lively and shockingly intimate.

You have to realize, these men were the cream of the crop in a dismal and brutal prison culture. They didn't have a stack of books they felt guilty for buying on Amazon and not reading. Any book they had was a treasure, and they read it passionately and wanted to talk about it.

In a prison, a conversation of any spiritual or emotional or intellectual depth is an amazing opportunity, and they took it seriously. More seriously than many of us take our conversations.

After all, we can always pick ours up later, so excuse me while I take this call on my cell phone, or half-listen to you while I check my e-mail, or order my coffee at Starbucks, or any of the million ways we distract ourselves with the things of this world.

To which Paul would say, "Set your minds on things that

are above"; in other words, on the things that really matter, because you won't find Jesus in Galilee or in Glen Ellyn or in Sing Sing if you're too distracted to look for him.

In fact, to a one, they had never experienced or seen the Internet, that's how long they had been inside.

"Tell us about what your church does for youth and teenagers," a prisoner asked me. And when I told them about all the programs we have at the church, the rotation workshops, the youth groups, the internships, the music, he said, "I wish I had had something like that." Another said, "That's the most important thing your church can do." And another said, "They have sixty kids in the classroom in my old neighborhood high school now. So what would Jesus think about that? What do pastors think about that?"

In the introductions each one said how many decades they had been there, and now I tried to guess their ages. I quickly did the math and then it hit me. They pretty much all seemed to be there for crimes they had committed when they were about eighteen years old. Of course they cared about youth ministry and education.

At the end of the seminar that day, the students asked if we could end the class early so that they could all get their books signed. One by one, they came forward, spelled their names, and asked me to write something in their books.

I usually sign books with the word "Blessings," but it seemed so strange to write that in an environment that showed so little sign of them. But it was also a place that needed blessings.

In prison, there are not many opportunities to come across gifts you can give to people on the outside. So a number of the men asked me to dedicate the book to someone else, in many cases a child, by now probably grown up. In one case, a prisoner wanted to give the book to his father, who was a pastor.

One man had forgotten his book in his cell, so he asked for a dedication on a scrap of paper that he planned to glue inside the book.

In my life, when I make a mistake like that, I can just run back into the other room and retrieve what I forgot, but not in prison. Prison is the place where there is no turning back.

Now, you could say, Well, prison is meant to be bad. You go there because you have done bad things.

Or you could say, as Jesus did, that every life has value, and that no soul is so corrupted that it is beyond hope.

Human beings are built with this divine blue chip for hope, with this inborn godly capacity to set our minds on the things above, and to see resurrection and new life even in the hardest situations.

As we were leaving, one man said, "Thank you for visiting us. We feel like nobody knows we are here. We couldn't believe you wanted to come and see people like us."

I assured him that the conversation had been of an outstanding quality, that I loved their humor, their wit, their insights, and that I wouldn't have traded the experience of meeting them for the world...Just as I was making it all seem a little too positive, he cut me off and said, "What you experienced here in the class, it's not like that out there. Out there," he said, gesturing to the other prisoners, "it's really bad."

I hated to see that man walk back out into the general population of the prison that day, adjusting his gait to convey a toughness that the new setting would demand. But I also recalled that he was one of the few who would be getting out soon, in thirty days. He planned to apply to seminaries and to pursue his dream of becoming a pastor, after three decades in the big house. If he could just set his mind on things above, and not get dragged down by the things of this world, he might have a shot at Easter, and a new life.

Which side would you bet on? Old life or new life? Well, statistically speaking, I've heard that the recidivism rate at Sing Sing prison is 60 percent. That means that the vast majority who get out commit another crime that lands them right back in jail. In other words, it's hard to keep your eyes focused on things above when the old life is all around you.

But then I thought of Paul, the brutal man whose heart Jesus claimed for love instead. And now we read his words on Sundays: "Set your minds on things that are above."

In Sing Sing, the recidivism rate goes down for every degree you get while you're inside, from high school GED to college course to the graduate program that I was visiting that day, where the recidivism rate was only 2 percent.

On the walls of the basement classroom were photographs of every graduating class for decades. The prisoners could tell you the stories of what the graduates were doing with excitement and enthusiasm, as if each one's redemption story was the gospel itself. Because, of course, it is.

In the depths of that tomb, they were keeping their minds on things above.

Christ has risen. He is risen indeed.

Chapter 9

Knitting Prayer Shawls and Baby Booties

O N TUESDAY NIGHTS, a group gathers in our church lobby to knit prayer shawls, baby blankets, and booties for the members of our congregation. The knitting ministry meets the same night as our church's governing board. So while we are in the conference room making big-picture decisions about the life of the congregation, just a few feet away on the couches other people are knitting for the sick, for new babies, or for those in need of any kind of healing. I think it's a nice combination of ministry on Tuesday nights, like a check and balance system for what leadership in the church is all about.

The knitters pray over the fruits of their labor before releasing them to whoever may need the blessing, and churches all over the world make prayer shawls. I still have the prayer shawl I received from my current church when I was sick, and I still have the prayer shawl I received from my former church when my mother passed away. I went on to inherit the prayer shawl her church made for her when she first fell ill. They all lie around my house as extra blankets in the family room, ordinary objects infused with prayer in the midst of our ordinary lives.

The prayer shawl didn't cure my mother's fatal illness. But there is no question in my mind that it was a conduit of healing. It remains a symbol to me of how all our churches are knit together by the Holy Spirit. New babies receive a handmade gift to keep them warm, blessed by prayer before it is given away. It's a symbol of a beautiful biblical metaphor that goes back many thousands of years. Psalm 139 reads, "For it was you who formed my inward parts; you knit me together in my mother's womb. I praise you, for I am fearfully and wonderfully made. Wonderful are your works."

It seems that people have been knitting for one another forever, perhaps ever since God, the original knitter, knit each one of us together in our mothers' wombs. So, indeed, we are wonderfully made.

When I feel discouraged, unworthy, or damaged, I like to remember that the Divine Knitter knit me together and made me wonderful. And when I feel cocky, superior, or smug, I remember that She did the same for everyone else, too.

Chapter 10

Confessions of a Picky Eater

I HAVE TO CONFESS that I am a picky eater. Not a righteous eater. Just a picky one.

I don't want to be. I want to be the kind of person who tries the octopus, who loves snails, and who eats whatever is offered. I want to be someone who visits a foreign country and accepts the gift of mysterious organs in the soup as an adventure.

But stop. I can't lie. I don't want to be that person at all. I think those people are crazy.

I have lists of things I will eat and things I won't, and the second list is way longer. And while I pretend to feel bad about it, and may give lip service to how much I know I am missing, it's not true. I don't think I am missing a thing. Everything on the list of things I don't like is there for a reason. I don't like it. Or at least I think I don't. And to my mind, that should be enough.

But Paul's advice to the early church was to eat whatever was put before you. He said, "If an unbeliever invites you to a meal and you are disposed to go, eat whatever is set before you without raising any question on the ground of conscience."

So why did he say that? I assume it was not simply to torture me.

In the days of the early church, there were all sorts of rules about who you could eat with and what you could eat. There was a sense that good people ate one way, and bad people ate another way.

But don't you relate to that? How many of you, when you go to the drive-through for something fried, sweet, milky, or greasy, make sure you throw away your junk food wrappers before anyone sees them? Would you be that panicked to have someone catch you eating a seaweed salad?

These days there are a lot of thoughtful people putting a lot of thought into what thoughtful people should eat. I know it's important to think about these things, but it's also important to think about people's feelings. I have seen people use their dietary rules like a battering ram, giving everyone who doesn't subscribe to them a case of heartburn.

We're a nation that has so many food choices, we have had to become the leader in food rules to keep ourselves in check. So let's not begrudge the vegetarian or the locavore or the omnivore with a dilemma. Let's not judge the big breakfast eater, the all-day snacker, or the person who thinks that if you eat it standing up and over the sink, it doesn't count.

Let's just sit at the table together in peace and give thanks.

God is great, God is good, let us thank God for our food. Amen.

Part III

COMMUNING

Chapter 11

Things I Am Tired Of

I AM TIRED OF HEARING people say stupid things in the name of Christianity I am tired of nutty, pistol-packing pastors who want to burn the Koran. I am tired of televangelists who claim that natural disasters are the will of God. I am tired of Christians who respond to the pain of disease with a lecture about behavior. I am tired of preachers who promise prosperity. As grumpy as it sounds, I am even tired of Tim Tebow.

I am also tired of people who say that they are privately spiritual but not religious, I am tired of people who have one bad experience with a church and paint the whole of Christianity with that brush. I am tired of celebrities who criticize the church for being patriarchal and homophobic but do nothing to support the churches that are not. I am super tired of Anne Rice.

I am tired of people who say they want a church like mine but cannot be bothered to attend one. And I am tired of people who criticize churches like mine and go somewhere else.

So I resonate with the angry words from letters to the early church that criticize shallow believers with itchy ears. I feel like I live in a society where stupid and simple spirituality always trumps the depth of a complex faith. We are a people of itchy ears, who depart from sound doctrine in favor of easy answers.

Perhaps I am really just tired of myself. In criticizing others in their faith, I hardly live up to the best in my own faith. Perhaps the people who irritate me the most are exposing my own false doctrines. And this is why I can't do this religion thing all by myself. This is why I need a community.

Chapter 12

No Sin, No Service

H AVE YOU EVER NOTICED that the restaurant where you least want to eat, the restaurant that looks the most unappealing and certainly the least elegant, is always the restaurant that has the sign NO SHIRT, NO SHOES, NO SERVICE?

And I find myself wondering, Has this been a problem for them in the past? Do people walk into these places and realize, "Oh no, I forgot my shirt. And my shoes too. But at least I've got my pants on"?

Is it a community-wide issue? Or is there one particular customer who keeps forgetting, and the sign is just for him?

In that case, it should say, "Jared, no shirt, no shoes, no service," so the rest of us don't get ideas.

When I'm in a restaurant like that, I am tempted to take

my shoes off, just to see what they'd do. Or then I think: "Are shoes and shirts the only deal-breakers here? What if you didn't have any pants on?"

But I've thought it through, and I sense that would be wrong. I suppose what they are trying to say with that sign is that although this is a casual place, there are limits. We don't just serve anybody. You have to have clothing on. Or at least these two specific items of clothing. Well, at least they put it out there. Most of society is not that honest. Groups of people have those signs in their heads, but outsiders never see them. You just perceive that there are rules and an order to things that some people seem to know and others don't.

So the new junior employee sits down at the cafeteria table and is horrified to discover he has plunked himself in the middle of senior management. Or a single man sits next to a beautiful woman only to be displaced by her husband for whom she was saving the seat, and he leaves embarrassed. Or a newcomer to the church sits in someone else's regular pew and can tell from a look that something is wrong, but what is it?

Or picture this moment: You enter the school cafeteria and freeze. You clutch your lunch and wonder. Where do I sit? Will I be welcomed? Will I be ignored?

This is the worst moment, but you will get through it. You will get through it because you have been the new kid before. Every couple of years, in fact, you have gone to a new school and faced this hideous moment.

But the noise from the lunch room hits you like a bomb.

It is so loud and so full, but for you it is so empty. All that chattering, shrieking, and laughing does not include you, and it never has. You are the outsider. You have nowhere to sit. You could turn around and spend the lunch hour in the bathroom, but then tomorrow you will have to deal with this again. Sit down, sit yourself down. It will be okay.

"Is someone sitting here?" you ask at a table with an empty seat or two.

A shrug. "Go ahead."

You remember your last school where, when you asked, "Is someone sitting here?" they said, "Sorry, it's taken." So you sat somewhere else and then spent the lunch hour looking at that still-empty seat, and the girls around it whispering to one another, saying, "That was mean," when their laughter indicated what it really was, to them: funny.

After that, you wondered if you would always eat alone at this school. And now, sitting here, living this moment one more time, you sit down and wonder: Will they talk to me? Will I ever eat with these people again?

"What's your name?" the girl I have joined at the table asks me. Another says, "Where did you move from?" And at her question, my heart fills with such gratitude that I fight to keep back the tears. They have welcomed me. I have a place to sit. I will not have to eat alone in the middle of a crowded room.

This was a scenario I went through every couple of years in my childhood, moving as we did from one place to another, a foreign correspondent's family, never staying in any one country very long. That internal first-day-in-the-lunchroom dialogue, I have it memorized and can recall it as if it were yesterday.

The desire to eat at a table with others seems to have been hardwired into human beings. But on the other hand, there aren't always people on hand.

Like so many people, there are times when I eat alone with the television on. I always read in health magazines that you shouldn't do that. Apparently, you should practice mindful eating, quietly savoring every morsel in solitude, thinking about the beautiful nutritional component of each bite, chewed one hundred times, so that the full flavor of the wheatgrass can enhance your spirit.

Oh, forget about it. You get your remote and channel surf your way through a wolfed-down meal, wishing you were eating the pizza they are advertising on TV, and therefore eating twice as much of whatever you have in front of you. Why do we do that? Why, in the privacy of our own homes, do we watch TV when we eat? Because when we're eating alone, it can feel lonely. We turn on the television for company. It goes back to the point that we like eating in the company of others.

We can't always pull it off today, but as human beings, we have always done it sometimes, gathered as groups to eat together, clearly enjoying it. Early art depicts it. The Last Supper clinched it. Eating at the table together has the capacity to be both very ordinary and earth-shattering.

In the communion liturgy from Luke's Gospel, we hear: "Their eyes were opened in the breaking of the bread." God was in action when they gathered at the table. None of that would have happened had the disciples each been eating alone.

But there is a social status element to all this as well. It is not just that we do not want to eat alone. We do not want to be seen as eating alone.

Whether it is the wedding banquet seating arrangement or walking into the corporate cafeteria, we notice who eats with whom. Where does your boss eat? Which groups of coworkers are clustered together? Do the union members sit on one side of the break room, the supervisor on the other? From our earliest nursery school memories of snack time to the seating chart at the retirement dinner, we know that these seating arrangements, formal and informal, mean something about who we are and where we are placed. And they say something about our society.

Let me give you an example from the local junior high school in my community, in the suburbs of Chicago. Those who set the rules for the school are aware of the social jockeying that takes place over where preteens eat, so they have come up with a solution, but it is one of those heavy-handed solutions that kills the gnat with the baseball bat and ends up damaging the table. When my son was in the sixth grade, I found out to my horror that they had no choice about where they sat. Lunchtime seating was assigned. By the Pharisees.

Now, those kids did have some small say in it. They let them choose where to sit at the beginning of the year, but from then on it was set. You had to sit with those people from that time on. It was an effort to reduce the chaos of the junior high lunchroom (well, good luck with that), but also an effort to make sure everyone had someone to sit with, that no one would be left out or excluded.

But how did the baseball bat kill the gnat and still damage the table? I'll tell you. Those early teen years are some of the most cliquish, times when good kids can be awfully hard on one another. You must remember those years yourself, when those social lines between groups are almost calcified. What a message to send during that developmental period: You are stuck in one social group. You cannot grow, you cannot change. Your social rut is set and you are stuck in it, from the first week of school on. It may seem minor. But that's a damaged social table, and it sets the stage for social stratification in adult life.

If Jesus had been a student in this school, he would not have been allowed to eat with the tax collectors and sinners. There would have been no opportunity for their redemption.

But I have a feeling that if Jesus had gone to this school, he would have broken that rule. For in his life, when he ate with the tax collectors and the sinners, he was breaking rules that were more rigid than that.

In Jesus' day, who you ate with mattered. Where you sat was not a casual affair. You were associated with the people you ate with. If they were good, upstanding people and they invited you to eat at their table, you were, by association, good and upstanding too. Add to this social pressure the fact that there were dietary laws that good, observant Jews followed, and those who did not follow them were considered unclean. So eating with the wrong people, who were not careful about such observances, would make you dirty by association.

Even worse, if people were sinners, known to the community as such, you definitely didn't want to eat with them. The only people who ate with the sinners were the other sinners, the people who had to share a table because no other table would have them.

So people kept track of these things. In Jesus' day, they weren't all eating in a school cafeteria; they were observing one another in small-town life. They kept track of who went into whose house, and who stayed for dinner, and who was invited and who was not invited. Everybody watched, and while there wasn't a sign hanging over the various dining room tables, you knew who would be served and who would not.

By the time I got to high school, in the suburbs of Washington, D.C., the last school I would attend before college, I had already been to nine other schools. So I knew how to read the lunchroom tables like an anthropologist. Technically, you were free to sit anywhere you liked, but not really.

There were the orchestra kids, the ethnic and cultural groupings, the loud kids, the quiet kids. One table featured a group that you never saw in any class, because they seemed to be present in school only for lunch.

There was another table that apparently you could eat at only if you were pretty. There was no sign posted, but there may as well have been. Only the handsome can sit here.

The nerds hung out together, talking about things the

people at that previous table would not have been able to understand anyway.

And then there was the back table, where any type of food could be turned into an aviation device, and weapons were crafted from straws, ketchup packets, and Tater Tots—tiny fried potatoes that functioned as missiles. You remember this table from your school days.

That's where I ended up, I must confess. Why? Because back when I was the new kid, they welcomed me.

But high school was the first place in my life where I actually got to start and graduate in one place, and so something remarkable happened over those three consecutive years. The lunch room ceased to be a place of terror and instead became for me a wonderful social buffet. And I decided not to be restricted to any one food group. I decided to cross-pollinate the lunch tables.

At first, when I would sit down at any of the aforementioned enclaves, I was stared at as if I had made a mistake. But gradually I got to know different people, make different friends, and realize that the cliques were not nearly as homogeneous as I had been led to believe.

There were smart students at the pretty table, and jocks at the orchestra table, and interesting stories everywhere. It was my grand experiment in lunch table infidelity and, like many forbidden things, it was fun.

One day at the nerd table, a guy who had seen me at the back table over the years said, "You know, Lillian, you're a lot less of a loser than you seemed to be."

I sympathized. "Yeah, you throw one Tater Tot and people think you're a moron."

"Well, you actually threw a lot of Tater Tots," he replied.

"Whatever. Dude, we've got to break down these walls."

It was a moment.

When Jesus was fishing for disciples, he was looking in some pretty shallow pools. These were not necessarily the best and the brightest. Not those voted most likely to succeed. At one point, he appears so desperate that the scripture tells us, "He saw a man called Matthew sitting at the tax booth; and he said to him, 'Follow me.' And the tax collector got up from his booth and followed him."

Now, tax collectors were the most hated group in the social system, not to be confused with government officials today. While we may not always enjoy paying our taxes, we hardly blame the guy who reads our tax returns, right?

But these New Testament tax collectors had sold out the Jewish people to the Empire, ratted out their own kind, extorting money for a bully just to pay their own bills. If there was anyone you could judge, it was a tax collector.

And as Jesus sat at dinner, all sorts of other tax collectors and sinners came and joined them. Because they had become a table with a culture. Not the nerd table, not the jock table, but the sinners' table. The rejects, the people no one else wanted to eat with. And there were Jesus and his disciples not just eating with them, but recruiting leaders from within their ranks.

The Pharisees, who were good and observant Jews, the ones who were most careful about the rules, saw this and must have said to his disciples, "Why does your teacher eat with tax collectors and sinners? Why isn't he sitting at his assigned table?" Because they were honestly baffled at this rule-breaking. They were genuinely worried that Jesus was making himself unclean. And he was, without apology.

"No shirt, no shoes, no service." Most of the world just isn't that direct. But the unspoken and unwritten rules are often the ones that cause the most pain.

Jesus turned the tables on that, by sitting at the wrong table. What made it the wrong table? The wrong people were sitting at it? Who are the wrong people? The ones who are not like us.

In the church I serve, we have long housed the homeless every Sunday night for seven months of the year, but we recently made the commitment to do it for all twelve months. Even though we live in an affluent suburb, our church hall is filled to capacity with about sixty men, women, and children in search of shelter.

But in making this change, to go year-round, we have received some feedback from the community around our church. There are concerns, because in the hours before and after the housing program, these guests do not really have anywhere to go. So they frequent the Starbucks and some of them panhandle, asking for money. Others push their carts filled with all their belongings around town, biding their time before the church doors are opened for dinner, or closed after breakfast. In other words, by wandering around a town they could never afford a home in, they do not respect the assigned seating arrangements.

In fact, some of the complaints I have heard center around the fact that the homeless have the nerve to sit on the bench outside the coffee shop, and by doing so, prevent others from sitting there who would not want to sit by someone like that.

It is as if, in this affluent suburb, there is an unspoken sign that says that if you pay enough money for your home, you should not only not have to sit next to a homeless person, you should not even have to see one.

And this attitude is not unique to my village, but pervades much of privileged culture.

To which Jesus and the church have a very clear answer that will not satisfy these people. The answer is this: in the world, there may be assigned seating, but in the kingdom of heaven there is not.

And so if we believe in that heavenly banquet, we ought to act like it, and live it out here. For Jesus and the disciples, there were no assigned seats at his table. All were welcome, particularly in their brokenness, for the church was born on the damaged consciences and rotten reputations of tax collectors, sinners, and people in need.

The church will always be criticized when it challenges the world on these issues. We will always be told that the barriers are there for a reason, that the rules are there to keep order, and that if we can keep to our own lunch tables, we will all be better off.

And the myth of that story is that you could keep all the sinners at their own table. Which is, of course, wrong, and also profoundly self-deceiving. Because there are sinners at every table.

You can argue with that. But I can say this for sure: there's a sinner at every table I sit down at, because it's me.

Often we read the stories about Jesus eating with the sinners as a cautionary tale against judging others. Do not be like those Pharisees, who exclude and divide. It's a good lesson to take away, but it's a lesson that puts us in the position of power and decision-making, where we think we belong.

Perhaps you should try reading this story like you're the tax collector. You're looking over the tables, wondering where you can sit down, and who will have you. You want a way out of your past mistakes and your sins. You want to live better. Perhaps you are circling around the edge of a church, wondering if there is a place for you in a religious community.

And there you see a man who sits with sinners, you, me, and the tax collector, and if there had been a sign above that table, it would have said, NO SIN, NO SERVICE. In other words, you need to be a sinner to eat at this restaurant. Which is just another way of saying, everyone is welcome. Church is a school for sinners, not a club of saints.

Chapter 13

The After-Tax Blessing

ARLY IN MY WORKING LIFE, I met with a financial planner. It seemed absurd since we were deeply in debt. We
had nothing to save, let alone invest. But a wise friend had
said this was just the time for such advice.

The planner reviewed our budget. We had been making
progress with our big credit card debt but there was more to
shovel out from under. We had also recently become tithers,
giving 10 percent of our income to the church. The two felt
connected in my mind. We had made progress on the debt
while growing in generosity. But I was embarrassed to tell that
to a financial planner. It is odd enough to give 10 percent to
your church as a member, but I was the pastor. I was essentially giving 10 percent of my salary back to my employer. I

knew he was going to tell us to be sensible, to give less away and to pay off the debt as soon as possible.

So when we got to the subject of charitable giving, I told him we were tithers.

"Tithers, huh?" he said. "Is that ten percent of after-tax income or pre-tax income?"

"After tax, of course," I said. After all, we were tithers, not fanatics. There was a long awkward pause, and I asked, "So what do you think of that?"

"It's fine," he said, "if all you want is an after-tax blessing!"

Then he laughed joyfully. Turns out, he was a tithing member of a church himself. His philosophy of financial planning had extreme generosity at its core. God had clearly sent a prophet our way, and he had issued us a challenge.

Chapter 14

Road Trip

RECENTLY, MY FLIGHT FROM O'Hare airport to Louisville was canceled due to bad weather. Ahead of me in the long line were all the people whose flights had been canceled the day before. It soon became obvious that we weren't going anywhere that day.

As people do, I began comparing notes about travel woes with a couple of guys next to me. One was eager to get home to his kids. The other had a long-awaited important medical appointment. I was supposed to give a talk that night. In seven hours. We all needed to get to Louisville.

I called my husband, Lou, to complain, and he did that annoying thing where he suggested that rather than complain, I might actually take charge and do something about my situation. He said, "It's a six-hour drive to Louisville from

99

Chicago, and you've got your car parked at the airport. Just get in right now and start driving." But there was a reason I had an airline ticket. I had never considered driving because I'm just not good at those long hauls. The longest drive I've ever done by myself was to Indianapolis and I felt that somebody should have been waiting for me at the end with a medal.

I wanted to get to my event, but I didn't feel like I could do it all by myself. And then it hit me. I was surrounded by people who might help me out, who might actually be longing for an invitation from a stranger. Here was that one guy who had been talking about how eager he was to get home and see his children after a long business trip and a day stranded at O'Hare. The other had said he had a really important medical appointment scheduled. And I had a car and an invitation I could make. To total strangers.

"Anyone want a ride to Louisville?" I asked, half jokingly.

"You bet," they both said at once.

Oh no. What had I just gotten myself into? What if they were ax murderers? Or worse, compulsive talkers?

"I hope you two are trustworthy people," I said, not entirely joking.

"I most certainly am!" said one, a middle-aged man with a short crew cut and a decisive manner. He whipped out his military ID with a salute. "Lieutenant colonel in the U.S. Army, on my way to Louisville for my final physical before I retire, after thirty-eight years of service."

So it looked like we three were off.

But just then, a young man standing behind us turned

bright red, as though he were getting up his courage to blow a house down. In a rush, he blurted out, "Okay, I can't believe I'm doing this, but, but, but…can I come too?"

This was becoming like ten clowns in a car. Who were these people and what had I gotten myself into? "Look, I'm a trustworthy person too," the third guy said. "In fact, I'm a Presbyterian minister." Well, how could I say no to that?

"You're a minister? Well, I'm a minister," I said. And we did that nerdy little minister dance that we do when we realize we're not the only ones.

The military guy looked hard at me and said, "*You're* a minister? Really?"

And the other guy said, "Wait till I tell my ex-wife I drove to Louisville with two ministers," and he shook his head as if this were going to be the longest trip of his life, listening to the two of us quote the Bible for six hours.

Once we were in the car, the terrible road conditions of sleet and ice made me nervous, but not nearly as nervous as my passengers, as I drove very slowly and fearfully.

One guy, the one about whom I realized I knew almost nothing, offered to take over the driving so many times it was almost rude. Finally I said to him, "Okay, we've heard what everyone else does for living. What do you do?"

"I'm a professional stunt car driver," he explained. Oh, the Lord does provide. At an Arby's, I turned over my keys and discovered that I had found the only driver capable of getting me to my speaking engagement on time, and he did it. With fifteen minutes to spare.

Later people told me I was crazy to go on this random road trip with strangers. But none of us would have made it there alone. Life's just better when we help one another. And it even ended up being fun.

In fact, the time just flew by. We heard one another's stories about previous marriages, what it's like to be a Mormon, life in the Presbyterian church, life in the military.

At the midpoint, we learned that the military guy owned no fewer than eighteen guns. "What are you going to do after you retire?" I asked. "Start a militia?" He didn't laugh. We moved on to other topics: the coolest sports cars, common race-car driving errors, and why bow hunting is the best way to get a deer.

And do you know, during that whole drive, we never once turned on the radio. Instead we all just talked. Four strangers at a banquet.

And now I have the beginnings of a really good joke. "Two ministers, a lieutenant colonel, and a stunt driver walk into a bar..."

There was a story a while back about a guy on Facebook who had about nine hundred friends, and he invited them all to a party. And you know the punch line: not one of them showed up.

It was an experiment to see whether Facebook friends really deserve the title of friend. People were struck at the irony that someone with hundreds of online contacts couldn't get one person to hang out with him.

Is our culture so disconnected that we are in constant touch electronically, but just too busy to see one another in person? Is this a modern problem? Or is it perhaps a problem of human nature that has been around forever? According to the Gospel of Luke, we are not the first generation to call each other "friends" but not have time for one another.

Jesus tells a story about a generous host who invited all kinds of people to a wonderful banquet. But all his good friends decided to decline the invitation. "No thanks," they said.

Some were busy, some wanted to work instead, and another guy had just gotten married, apparently to a wife who wouldn't let him leave the house. The host got so annoyed, and perhaps even had his feelings so hurt, that he went out and invited total strangers to come to his party and eat all his good food.

He told his servant, "Go out at once into the streets and lanes of the town and bring in the poor, the crippled, the blind, and the lame."

Let's get a whole crew of misfits together, people who don't fit in, or who don't know one another, who are not part of the in crowd, let's mix up all the cliques and have a party. It would be like the island of misfit toys.

Last weekend, I was on another kind of trip, this one not with strangers but to see people I know well, my extended family in South Carolina. And my cousin, who is like a sister to me, asked me if I would go to church with her, which of course I was eager to do, since I don't get to do that very much. But my cousin has recently converted to a new form of Christianity, to a very high church with a sung Latin mass, beautiful music, incense. This is a very traditional smells-and-bells church, where mass, or communion, is celebrated every week as the center and high point of the service. And as different as it was from my own church, I was truly enjoying every part of it, in its strange and different beauty, marveling that God can work in so many different forms.

Then, in the bulletin, I noticed a paragraph that said something to the effect that the communion was open only to members of the church. This is not an issue of hospitality, the note said, but a recognition of the brokenness of the church and our divisions. So nonmembers were not supposed to come forward to receive communion. Instead, we were expected to pray to draw closer to Christ, the implication being that we were too far away already. And when I read it, the joy I had been feeling at the service disappeared, and I felt belittled. Sort of rejected. Well, not sort of. Really.

And then I thought of the story of the generous host who invited everyone to his banquet. And I decided that the Bible gets to trump any one paragraph in a bulletin, and I decided to forget I had even seen it. I took communion that day, quietly and anonymously, and the church didn't fall down around me, because in the end, I believe we are all one church. And the joy of the service returned.

All our denominations bring different treasures and gifts to the table. And no one branch gets to own communion. I wasn't willing to sit in the pew while everyone else went to the banquet, because I don't think anybody should have to do that.

And as my inspiration, I went to my favorite Catholic theologian of the fourth century, who said wise words to the church that still inspire and challenge me today. It was St. Augustine who said: "In essentials unity, in nonessentials diversity, in all things charity."

My fourteen-year-old daughter was so excited to have a French exchange student that she signed us up for two of them. The day of the arrival, all her friends came over to make signs to welcome them. We waited in the sleet and snow of the school parking lot for an hour and a half before getting word that the bus was about to arrive. Jumping around in the cold, French students searched the crowd for the sign with their name, and then politely kissed the cheek of their host. But no one was coming toward our sign.

My daughter walked into the fray and soon I caught sight of her talking to an awkward-looking teenage boy. I rushed over and announced, "I'm Abigail's mother. Welcome to America!" He looked awkward and shy, but I threw open my arms and enveloped him in a big hug.

"Ma, that's not our student!" Abigail informed me, rolling her eyes as the French boy extracted himself from my grip. But in the end, who cares? I didn't care.

It doesn't matter whose we are. We all deserve a big welcome.

Chapter 15

The Special Occasion

I REMEMBER THE NEW YEAR'S EVE of the new millen-
nium, which would turn out to be the last New Year's
Eve I would get to spend with my mother. We had decided
to go to a party that was being held at her wonderful church.
Before leaving, my mother pulled out a bottle of very fine
champagne, which she had been saving for years for just the
right occasion. With fanfare she suggested that we pop it
open and drink it together, which we all thought sounded
perfect.

Everyone except her husband, that is. "No, absolutely not,"
he said. "We're saving that for a special occasion."

"New Year's Eve is a special occasion," she said. But of
course New Year's Eves had come and gone in the past and
this bottle had not been opened on those previous occasions.

They argued over this matter and ended up not opening the bottle.

But it turns out that by then her illness was past the point of treatment, and I don't believe she ever drank it. She never got to kill that fatted calf.

Looking back, this was a conflict between family members that is very similar to the one in the story Jesus told about the prodigal son. When should you and when should you not kill the fatted calf? Do you wait for the right and perfect time to celebrate, or do you let the celebration transform the imperfection of the moment? It's an ancient question that we still ask today.

Jesus spoke often in parables, making his point by telling a story. Sometimes, there was a situation that prompted his telling a story. Apparently he was sitting at a table eating with sinners, and it made some of the holier people, the ones who tried to be perfect, well, it made them angry. And it also made them question his leadership. And so to respond to that, he told the story of the prodigal son.

There's a rebellious son who runs off and wastes his parents' money on drunkenness, out of control gambling, and prostitutes until the money dries up and he's reduced to living with pigs and eating their slop.

Finally, he got desperate enough to come home where, lo and behold, instead of being met with scolding or shame, he was received with dancing and singing, and the slaughtering of the fatted calf they had been saving up for a special banquet. He was greeted with a huge spontaneous celebration and the warm embrace of a father who had let go of all judgment and was just glad to have his son back at home.

But this story is not without its tension. Not everybody thought it was time to celebrate and to kill the fatted calf. I'm guessing the fatted calf wasn't particularly happy about it, but the story focuses on the feelings of a very human character: the older brother. He's the one who creates the real tension in the plot. Lurking in the wings of the welcome home celebration, the dutiful older brother steamed and boiled with resentment. Once again his younger brother was not just getting away with bad behavior, but seemed to be rewarded for it.

I've looked at people with that kind of resentment before and, be honest, you have too. You've asked yourself, "Why am I struggling at work and that jerk seems to be rushing by me on the career ladder, coasting through life?" And perhaps you, like the older brother, have wished for a different plot turn for someone else, one that seems just a little more fair, or at least logical.

For example, the father could have said, "You know what, son, I am so glad to see you home. After all those years of irresponsibility, moving out to Vegas and losing all our money, your issues with addiction . . . after all that you're finally home, I'm so happy I've decided to order us all a pizza. A medium. But can you at least cover the tip?

"And then, in a few years, after you get your college degree, I'll take you out somewhere nice, a sit-down restaurant. And after law school, after you get a job your mother and I can really be proud of, I'll have a fatted calf waiting for that banquet. But you're not getting that right off the bat and for no good reason. For now, be glad you're getting the pizza."

He could have said that. In fact, many parents do. It's not bad parenting, the incentive system. Besides, let's be realistic. What did lie in store for the son after he got home? Based on what he would go on to do, did he really deserve a banquet and all that fanfare?

You don't go straight from that dissolute lifestyle to law school. You don't go straight from gambling debt to being the guy who discovers the cure for diabetes. You don't go straight from eating pig slop to figuring out how to solve the world hunger problem. No, the prodigal son probably got home, ate the fatted calf, enjoyed the banquet, and then went down to his old bedroom in his parents' basement and played video games for the next six months while he doubled the family's grocery bill.

So why didn't the father save that fatted calf for a better occasion, or perhaps even use it as a little incentive to push this underachiever toward something better? That's what the older brother was thinking. Let's postpone the celebration for when he's earned it and hold off for now. This was just not enough of a special occasion.

But the father didn't want to hold off and everyone celebrated while his oldest son sulked.

It's been said that resentment is like swallowing poison and waiting for the other guy to die. I think you could say that killing the fatted calf is like celebrating and waiting for the other guy to experience joy.

There's never a perfect time to celebrate. But there is limited time in life to celebrate.

One very sad summer, I sat in the Washington National Cathedral as our family gave thanks for the short lives of two extraordinary young men, two brothers, Stone and Holt Weeks, killed in a car accident that July—both of them in their twenties. They had made such a difference in so many people's lives that their own church wasn't big enough for their memorial service. The cathedral opened its doors instead and the place was packed. If those two amazing young men were to walk through the door today, there would be no end to the celebration that would take place. No end.

The scripture says that the father of the prodigal son thought the boy was dead, and then thought that he had returned to life. Of course he was welcomed home with everything the family had to give. Of course. What better occasion could he possibly be waiting for?

"What are you waiting for?" the little girl asked her mother. "When are we ever going to use our fancy china?" She had been asking her mother why they never ate in the formal dining room, why they never used the china her parents had received for their wedding, why they never pulled out the silver. "That's for a special occasion," her mother replied, and looked sternly at her. "Don't ever touch this."

Years later, the daughter, now a teenager, asked, "But what

are you waiting for?" By now it had become an accusation. It seemed to sum up all the daughter's frustrations with a family that never seemed to be able to celebrate.

Everything was always done in moderation and it was always fair. The parents prided themselves on that. You got good grades, you got privileges. If you didn't do your chores, those were ratcheted back. The house was neat and orderly because the expectations were clear. If there was one piece of cake left, they didn't even ask who wanted it; they just carefully cut it into equal pieces, one bite for each kid.

"Just once, couldn't one person get to eat the whole extra piece of cake?" the teenager wondered. Just once, couldn't someone lavish attention on me, not because of my grades, or what I've achieved, but just because?

It seemed like the special occasions never came.

When they did occasionally pull out the good china, it was for some formal meal that seemed stripped of joy. The family seemed to want these occasions to end quickly. They did not feel special. It was as if they were so out of practice at special occasions, they just weren't any good at them. Her mother worried that someone would drop a plate. "Those plates are irreplaceable," she said. "They don't make that pattern anymore."

The girl stopped asking her mother to get out the good china. It wasn't worth it.

When she married, the young woman didn't get herself any fancy china. What was the point? But after a few years, she inherited her mother's. And she vowed that she would actually use it. In the beginning, she pulled it out often for birthdays and for dinner parties and didn't worry about a plate breaking. But with a baby, then a toddler, and the chaos of everyday life, the good china got put away until one day her own small daughter noticed it in the cupboard and asked, "Wow, can we use this tonight?" And before she could catch herself, the mother said, "No, it's for a special occasion. Don't touch it."

"Isn't today a special occasion?" the little girl asked. She was too young to know that adults like to save up and wait for such things. She was too young to have learned that you earn them.

And her mother stopped and looked around her. The kitchen was covered in dirty pots and pans from an afternoon of kids baking and playing at the house. The dog was once again eating out of the dishwasher. Her husband had just walked in and was grabbing a beer after a long commute, but she still needed to get some strange bubbling plastic container out of the microwave and its contents into her daughter's stomach before youth group at church, and after that, she still had twenty or thirty work e-mails to catch up on before this Wednesday night was done.

But the messy house had been full of laughter. It held more spirit and joy than anything she had known as a child, because sometimes the people with the coldest parents end up with a particular gift for warming a nest. And she had grown a faith that reminded her to stop and give thanks for the small things in the present. And in that moment, that's exactly what she did. She looked at her daughter, changing and growing

112

so quickly, and realized that her presence in this house and in this world was temporary, and said to herself, and then to God, "But that child is irreplaceable. They don't make that pattern anymore."

She pulled out some plates from the dusty set of good china and put them out on the messy kitchen counter. Surveying the detritus of this, another typical chaotic, rushed, and messy Wednesday night, she looked her daughter in the eye and said, "You're right, this is a very special occasion."

And together they set the table with the same love that God sets the table for you and for me, and for all the rest of her prodigal, irresponsible, precious, and irreplaceable children.

That is the story that Jesus told the people who criticized him for sitting at the table with sinners.

My mother was a magnificent entertainer. There was something about a meal at her house that topped everything. It was not the cooking, by the way. Sometimes that was delicious, but other times the gravy was likely to have burned on the stove, or the chicken was frighteningly undercooked, or the meal came out an hour late, blackened and crunchy. And that was just the green beans. But there was something about being at that table that pointed you toward abundance. You knew you were special, that someone had set the table for you, put on festive music, and killed the fatted calf, even if the food was strange. There were flowers on the table and candles— the hostess's motto was, "Well, it may not be good but it'll certainly be fancy." You knew you had been well served.

One night, my mother came out more than an hour late, dressed to the nines in a sparkly outfit a couple sizes too small, red high heels clicking across the floor, holding, on a giant tray, a magnificent roasted duck. It was a brand-new recipe for her. We had waited a long time for the meal, but now it appeared. It was hard to find the duck on the plate, for in her enthusiasm for her project she had gone heavy on the garnish. It was like a parsley explosion of culinary enthusiasm, a product of a long day's work, cheerfully given.

But then, somehow, the combination of all the greenery, the grease of the duck, and a fold in the carpet just underneath her high-heeled shoes came together in the perfect storm. And as she tripped, the duck she had spent the whole day preparing went flying across the room, landed where once its tail feathers had been. It skidded across the floor only to stop on the muddy doormat in the front hall, a brown trail of grease, gravy, and parsley garnish in its sad wake.

The hostess had a moment when tears welled up, and there was a collective gasp among the guests. You could see she was thinking about how she would be judged. My mother knew from experience how easy people find it to mock a person when things go wrong. But then it was as if a new spirit came upon her, and she pulled her little shoulders back, marched over to the duck on the doormat, stooped down, and picked it up as she announced to the group, "Let me just throw this duck away in the kitchen, and I'll be back in just a minute with the *other* duck."

And a few minutes later she made another grand entrance,

this time avoiding the crease in the carpet. The duck was even more heavily disguised in garnish, to cover the bruises, for of course, as we all knew, there was no other duck. This was it.

But the holy spirit of hospitality was such that without a word, it was as if the guests collectively decided to replace the world's petty practices of judgment and critique with a spirit of generosity. And we sinners all ate well at the table that night, feasting less on the damaged duck than on the grace that was served to both an embarrassed hostess and to her hungry guests.

Our hostess is gone from this world, so she's the one I always picture ushering me into the afterlife, with a plate of burned hors d'oeuvres and some fatted calf.

There we'll all be, gathered around the banquet table, not just the perfect people but also the other 99.9 percent of humanity. The prodigal son and his hard-partying buddies, the joyful father, the oldest son, and his responsible friends too, they're all there along with you, and me, and my cousins, and all those who have gone before.

And suddenly, in the midst of this banquet, there's a moment when we finally realize that all the jockeying for position we did in our lives, all the resentment, competition, and score keeping, is meaningless because we didn't earn our place at this abundant table, but got here through God's extravagant grace.

And Jesus, well used to eating with sinners, now serves us in person, the bread, the wine, the fatted calf, and the other duck. "Now this," he says, "is indeed a special occasion."

Part IV
WANDERING

Chapter 16

Hog Time

THERE'S A FOLKSY STORY about a busy young man who came up behind a poor farmer who was taking his hog to market. The market was a few miles away, and as the young man walked briskly, he got closer to the slow-moving farmer and caught sight of the spectacle. The farmer was picking up this enormous hog, carrying it about twenty feet, and then dropping it in exhaustion. Then the farmer would wipe the sweat from his brow, take a few minutes to catch his breath, and pick up the hog again.

When the young man caught up with the farmer he had to comment. "That is the most inefficient way to get a hog to market I've ever seen. The market's half an hour away but this is going to take you all day. Why don't you just let the hog walk?"

To which the farmer replied, "Shucks, son. Time ain't nothing to a hog!"

Which one had it together, the hurrying young man or the farmer? It all depends on how you define and value time. Who are you in that story? Are you the rushing young man, full of concerns for efficiency? Or are you the old farmer, going about things your own way without much sense?

Or how about this, what if you're the hog? What if all of us are the hogs?

Then God's the old farmer.

God picks us up, carries us a little way on the journey, and then puts us down for a rest. Then God picks us up and carries us a little farther, and stops, giving us small increments on the journey, one piece at a time, in the hope that we might stop focusing on where we are going and instead notice where we are.

After all, time ain't nothing to a hog.

Chapter 17

Speaking in Tongues

I HAVE A RECURRING NIGHTMARE about the final exam on which my college graduation depends. Thinking I am prepared, I open a blue booklet only to discover that I am being tested in a language I do not know. I try to explain that there has been a terrible mistake, but the proctor's answer is unforgiving. Sent back to my chair to take a test that I have no hope of understanding, let alone passing, the number 2 pencil shakes limply in my sweaty hand.

Unfortunately when I wake up, instead of feeling relief, I recall real-life experiences that were all too much like my dreams.

After studying French for five years, I opened the booklet for a college placement test and still understood nothing. Forging ahead, telling myself this was merely a result of nerves, I did my very best and ended up placing into ... first-year French. I'd like to pretend that it's just test-taking anxiety, but I have the same panic reaction when confronted with a French menu.

My college had a fluency requirement, so I decided to try Spanish instead. For years I was invisible under the back row "credit/no credit" radar, until at the end of senior year, my teacher suddenly decided to call on me in class. *"Como te llama?"* she asked, and for the first time my eyes made direct contact with hers. I had no idea what she was saying.

Today, my own two teenagers have no shortage of criticism for the world in general, but these days, their most piercing sneers are reserved for lip-synchers, the starlets and rocker wannabes who perform by moving their lips while a canned sound system provides the music. Britney Spears and Ashlee Simpson are the lip-synchers of our day, but in my younger years, it was the famous male pop duo Milli Vanilli, who tearfully confessed that although they looked like models and had achieved pop chart success, they had never sung a note of their own music in public.

"Como te llama otra vez?" the Spanish teacher repeated. She was asking me what my name was. After all, given my total lack of class participation, how would she know? But I still had no idea what she was asking, and knew only the cold dread of one about to be exposed.

"Lillian," the person sitting next to me said to the teacher. *"Se llama Lillian."*

"Gracias," said the teacher to the student who answered on my behalf. And that was it.

122

My brief brush with conversational Spanish had ended, and I lived to see another credit. Barely. But the nightmares remain.

So it was with a sense of wonder that two decades later I found myself sitting at our local community college in a class titled Introduction to Conversational Spanish. You don't end up middle-aged in a noncredit continuing ed course because you are a linguistic genius—everyone else in that class had a story like mine.

As we students introduced ourselves, we marveled that ten people who had never met before could all have the same recurring nightmare. But we also shared another story, the story of the church.

Some people had been on mission trips and returned with a desire to learn the language of the people they had visited. Another person's church had started a Spanish language worship service, and she had wandered in. Others were hoping to go on a mission trip, and in that hope, they were willing to try to learn a language once again. That was my story. I had signed up to build houses in Guatemala, and I had six months to learn a few words of the language.

On Pentecost, the followers of Jesus suddenly understood one another's languages. They spoke across the boundaries that had separated them with such power that people thought they were drunk. Today, some people live that out by speaking in tongues. Others sign up for a Spanish class and then wonder, "What...was I drunk?"

At the final class we listened to one another's oral presentations. I learned about Sammy the black pug, an Italian cousin who came to visit, and a castle in Germany that is an exact replica of the one at Disneyland. Who knew? I actually understood and followed a tale about a bird watching club's trip to Ohio to see a magnolia warbler en route to Canada. And let me be honest, that's a tale you would have lost me on, had it been in English.

I also heard about AIDS orphans in Kenya, an Anglican church in Mexico, and house-building projects around the world. Almost everyone struggling to conjugate verbs was there because of some church. In a world of lip-synching pop stars and glitzy productions, our little class seemed remarkable for its lack of finesse but the fullness of its witness.

It could only be faith that got us in the door on the first day. Against the wisdom of experience, we were back in the classroom that haunted our dreams, back to those grammar charts where we had all known defeat, but now hoped for victory.

Como te llama, otra vez?
Me llamo Lillian.

Chapter 18

The Poor Are Not Lucky

A WELL-DRESSED WOMAN at a religion conference told me that she had learned that it was harder for rich people to experience God's love than the poor. "The poor," she explained, "have so little that they have to rely on God's love so much more. They just seem so much happier." This was presumably why she delighted in mission work overseas, where the poor were "just so grateful."

She was inspired by the people she served, saying, "They offer me so much more than I offer them." Well, at least that last part I could imagine to be true, but not for the reasons she imagined.

She continued to explain that the people who have less, have less to worry about, and that was why they were closer to God. "In some ways, I truly envy them," she said. "It is just easier for them to experience God's grace." For that reason, she believed that it was more worthwhile for her to offer her presence than her money.

I have heard rich people say that "the poor are lucky" before. But I have yet to hear a poor person say it.

Yes, Jesus does say that we get closer to God by giving away what we have. But the poor do not get closer to God by having less. Most people in the world are not poor by choice. They are poor because other people have more than their fair share. Whole nations steeped in poverty are not an accident of fate. Whole nations who enjoy most of the world's wealth are not God's will.

"Generosity begets generosity," Jesus assures us. Generosity ought to inspire others to be generous. Mission trips are miraculous faith-filled pilgrimages when they alert us to the injustice in the world and inspire us to be generous and to change things. Mission trips are self-serving vacations when we come back thinking that the poor we met overseas are the lucky ones.

We can admire the poor people we meet, and we can respect them, but to call them lucky is ridiculous. When generosity begets stupidity it wasn't really generosity to begin with. But when generosity begets more generosity, it is the real thing.

I have always loved this Benedictine prayer: Dear God, give bread to those who are hungry and a hunger and thirst for justice to those who have plenty. Amen.

Chapter 19

Please Stop Boring Me

O N AIRPLANES, I DREAD the conversation with the person who finds out I am a minister and wants to use the flight time to explain to me that he is "spiritual but not religious." Such a person will always share this as if it is some kind of daring insight, unique to him, bold in its rebellion against the religious status quo.

Next thing you know, he's telling me that he finds God in the sunsets. These people always find God in the sunsets. And in walks on the beach. Sometimes I think these people never leave the beach or the mountains, what with all the communing with God they do on hilltops, hiking trails, and... did I mention the beach at sunset yet?

Like people who go to church don't see God in the sunset! Like we are these monastic little hermits who never leave the church building. How lucky we are to have these geniuses inform us that God is in nature. As if we don't hear that in the psalms, the creation stories, and throughout our deep tradition.

Being privately spiritual but not religious just doesn't interest me. There is nothing challenging about having deep thoughts all by oneself. What is interesting is doing this work in community, where other people might call you on stuff or, heaven forbid, disagree with you. Where life with God gets rich and provocative is when you dig deeply into a tradition that you did not invent all for yourself.

Being privately spiritual but not religious has become the norm in American culture, and has even made its way into the culture of some of our churches. So while I can't stop these people from talking to me on the airplane, can I at least inform them that they are boring?

Thank you for sharing, spiritual but not religious sunset person. You are now comfortably in the norm for self-centered American culture, right smack in the bland majority of people who find ancient religions dull but find themselves uniquely fascinating. Can I switch seats now and sit next to someone who has been shaped by a mighty cloud of witnesses instead? Can I spend my time talking to someone brave enough to encounter God in a real human community? Because when this flight gets choppy, that's who I want by my side, holding my hand, saying a prayer, and simply putting up with me, just like we try to do in church.

Chapter 20

Animals in the Airport

ONE OF THE STRANGER THINGS about air travel is being cut off from nonhuman creatures. When you get on an airplane, you are not only leaving behind the people you know, but perhaps a dog, a cat, or a goldfish as well. At the airport, you swim in a sea of people, but almost never see an animal. Cut off from the outside air, the trees, and the grass, air travel is just not pet territory.

I realized this when I encountered an exception. Flying in to a landing strip in Botswana, where our family was going for a safari, the animals were already waiting for us on the landing strip. As we bounced on air pockets, in a tiny plane with all the room and power of a Ford Escort with wings, safari guides on the ground ran up and down the runway to chase away the giraffes.

The giraffes were on a more leisurely schedule that day, and weren't too worried about these tiny human beings waving and shouting at them, but then a lion approached and they decided to move a bit more aerobically toward the jungle. But they still didn't flee in a panic. They looked back at the lion as they left, as if to say, "Hey, we're cool. We were leaving anyway."

But through all this animal diplomacy, the toy plane just kept heading in. Gratefully, by the time the plane landed, or rather fell out of the sky in exhaustion, the lion had decided to leave the runway and follow the giraffes, because, hey, he was going to do that anyway. But throughout the whole adventure, I realized that part of what made it unforgettable was not just the animals themselves, but that we had seen them somewhere they were not supposed to be, at a time we didn't expect them to be there. You don't look out the airplane window for lions and giraffes. But from now on, I may.

It's not just modern people who have struggled with the issue of where humans should be and where animals should be. The Bible is full of images about the kingdom of heaven where animals get together in strange partnerships, like the lion and the lamb that lie down as cuddly friends ready for the next popular cute pet video on YouTube.

In other places, that same prophet Isaiah talks about heaven as a place where we will be safe from animals, where a jackal's haunt will become a swamp, with a holy highway running through it where no lions shall pass.

We human beings have this ancient preoccupation with

animals, with being hunted. Maybe that's why today, whenever we are trying to do something really important, like make a $250 million airplane, weighing tons, take off and fly through the air, we would rather the animals scat and stay gone. We have made that our own holy highway, where jackals and lions do not rule, and they can't even get a ticket. Airports are human territory.

For that reason, on the rare occasion someone travels with a pet, it gets a lot of attention. People ooh and ah over the little dog that gets carried through the security line, wild eyed and nervously shaking. And they always seem to be little dogs, don't they? I can't see maneuvering a hundred-pound mutt in and out of one of those little designer doggie cases that fits under a seat.

In airports, you see the big dogs working. They might be walking with a blind person, allowed to enter restaurants and bathrooms, and other places where dogs seem surprising. Big dogs in airports also work with the folks in security and police uniforms, sniffing for drugs and explosives. And they do always seem to be big dogs, don't they? Have you ever seen a Yorkshire terrier sniffing for drugs, or a Chihuahua? It seems that at airports, dogs have their roles. The little ones get carried onto the plane in luxury and the big ones work.

Or they fly in the luggage compartment. I am always touched at the luggage check to see some enormous dog carrier get carted off with the luggage. Inside you see the big, sad eyes of a nervous dog being separated from its owner. I remind myself that this is not really a tragic scene but a loving one.

Someone loves this big mutt enough to fly it across the country. This dog may be about to get a new yard, a new living room to shed fur all over, and a new set of squirrels to chase across the neighborhood. This dog is scared now, but we who are watching this scene know that he must be very loved. The dog can't see it, but I trust he will know it soon enough. Love waits for him on the other side of this hard journey.

Those traveling and working dogs are not all that different from us humans. When someone says good-bye to us, we are scared and wonder where we are being sent off to, even when we can read the destination on our ticket. We are sometimes nervous in the security line, even though we can understand the words being spoken to us. The dogs in the airport get our attention because they display the emotions that we cover up. They shake nervously, while we act calm. They bark, when we try to keep our voices low and even. They look scared in their cages, while we try to appear confident. Their cages are visible, whereas our cages are invisible. We may feel as trapped as they do, but no one knows.

I think God watches us like we watch those pets. Out of place in the airport, or out of place in the world, God observes it all. God sees our nervousness, our fears, and hears our barking. And when we're being shipped off in a carrier, God has a sense of the destination and wants us to know we're going to be okay. But we can't see all that. We don't know where on earth we are going. And so God is the gentle stranger who offers a kind word, a pat, a drink of water, and then sends us on our way, wanting us to know we are loved, even when we feel like a fish out of water, or as out of place as a dog in an airplane.

Or a bird for that matter. In the bathroom of an airplane. Yes, it happens.

I waited awkwardly in the line for the bathroom, but the person in there was taking forever. And what strange noises were coming out of there. Were there two people in there having a conversation? When the door opened I was caught in a cloud of feathers. A woman came out with an enormous cockatoo on her arm, and it was talking in a human voice. The flight attendant stepped up awkwardly. "You were not supposed to take that bird out of its carrier," he said.

The woman ignored the flight attendant and sat in her seat with the large bird on her lap. I looked inquisitively at the flight attendant, to silently ask the question with my eyes, "What on earth is going on?"

"It's a therapy bird," he informed me. "So it's allowed on the plane. But we didn't think she would let it out of the cage."

The woman overheard this and turned to say, "Yes, it is a therapy bird, and I need it to go with me everywhere I go. I have a note from my doctor."

One passenger asked another quietly, "Is a therapy bird like a Seeing Eye dog?"

"I think so," the other passenger said. "But I don't think that woman is blind."

"Maybe the bird is blind," the first passenger said, "and she's providing some assistance to the bird."

"Helloooo," said the bird.

"All I know is that I don't want to see that bird start flying around in here."

Suddenly the woman jumped up and stood in the line for the bathroom once again, just behind me. The bird's head was jutting back and forth, like he was deciding whether or not to peck my shoulder or to fly headlong into the cockpit door.

"You really can't take that bird with you to the bathroom again," the flight attendant said.

"Well, I'm not taking him with me," the woman said, as the large bird spread its wings and suddenly flutter-jumped off her arm and onto her shoulder, one wing slapping against my face. The rest of us in the bathroom line flinched away, almost falling into the laps of the people in the aisle seats, as they in turn leaned into the window seats. Nobody wanted to be too close to that bird.

"You are obviously taking it with you," the flight attendant said. "Everyone can see it right there on your shoulder."

"No, I am not taking it with me to the bathroom," she said. "I have already just used the bathroom, as you well know. This time, my bird is taking *me* with him. Now, *he* needs to use the facilities."

With that, the three of us in line all had one thought. It really wasn't that long a flight. We could wait and go at the airport.

The bird squawked in triumph as we retreated to our seats. "Helloooo!"

This reminds me of a story I heard about a man who had a parrot that had a terrible attitude and an even worse vocabulary. He tried to change the bird's behavior by speaking softly and saying only loving and encouraging things, but still the bird continued to squawk awful things at everyone in the home.

At one point the owner finally lost his temper and, just to get some peace and quiet, threw the parrot into the freezer. The parrot yelled insults and foul language for a while and then was suddenly silent.

"Oh no," he thought, because he didn't want to hurt the bird. Pulling open the door, he was relieved to see that the parrot was just fine. In fact, the parrot said very sweetly, "I want to sincerely apologize for my bad language, my mean attitude, and anything I have done to annoy you."

The owner was amazed at the transformation. But then the parrot added, "And now, if I may be so bold, can I ask what the turkey did?"

That story is funny because it taps into a deep tension about how or whether human beings and animals can interact. Obviously we can't really converse, but there are ways in which we can be in very close quarters with creatures that are profoundly different from us, and yet created by the same source.

There's one airport my husband travels in and out of in Detroit where somehow birds have nested and they fly around in the terminal. They have tried to take care of the issue but the birds keep showing up and multiplying. They eat the fast food crumbs, and the bugs in the potted plants. And they make their nests in the cold modern ceilings. As hard as we humans try to control our spaces, nature takes hold with a stubborn spirit. It is as if we are not meant to be cut off from one another. There, the birds fly and dip like aviators on a beautiful day, all within the confines of a Midwestern airport. There, the birds in the airport get the last word. I guess they have yet to lay eyes on a frozen turkey.

A few years back, our church began to hold an annual Blessing of the Animals service. If airports are not very pet friendly, churches are less so. At least in airports you see the occasional animal, but very rarely in a church. So I will never forget that first service we held and the oddness of it all.

On a lovely fall Saturday morning, by the side entrance to the chapel, greeters waited on the lawn with dog biscuits, cat treats, and bowls of water, as the pets and their human friends got to know one another. A few dogs sniffed and peed on the church sign, which raised a few eyebrows. But from a dog's point of view, what greater tribute?

Coming into the chapel was quite a scene, as pet owners struggled to keep their animals calm. Leashes were pulled tight but still the dogs wanted to sniff one another in a manner that was rather risqué for church. But given that it was a first worship experience for them, we decided to suspend the "no sniffing the other parishioners" rule that day.

Our young associate minister began to preach his sermon, holding his darling little Persian cat in his arms, and I don't know which one of them was having a better hair day. But then that little blow-dried cat took one look at my huge, slobbering Lab mix mutt and she started hissing. Bruno responded with a cross between a growl and a tortured moan, which I translated as "Please, Mommy, let me eat it!" Every church has its conflicts, but I did not want to mediate the wreckage of watching the senior minister's dog eat the associate minister's cat. I held Bruno tight and tried to get him to stop lunging toward the cat like it was a snack.

And then all the animals were at it, chiming in with all kinds of strange noises that had not been heard in the chapel since the last senior high school lock-in. What a cacophony.

It remains in my memory one of the most joyful worship services I have ever attended. The animal noises made the human beings crack up in laughter. I imagine God delighted in the hilarity. Together, all God's creatures, we were making a joyful noise to the Lord.

At one point, the whole world was safe for animals. Now their territory is constricted. Human beings control so much of the landscape and we have huge areas where animals rarely go—schools, hospitals, stores, churches. So I like to think of the sight of an animal in the airport as a special gift. We get a glimpse of nature in a sterile place. We get a dose of animal instinct in a place where we all have to behave ourselves. It's as odd as hearing a dog bark in church, and just as wonderful.

My hope is that when I finally get to the holy highway, it won't be free of jackals and lions, but will have room for everyone on the road. We'll all be safe, we'll all be redeemed, the therapy bird, the rude parrot, the Persian cat, the hungry dog, Bruno, and you and I, all of us in search of a home, every one of us, finally adopted by the one who has owned us all along.

Chapter 21

Immigrants Like Us

W E NEVER KNEW MUCH about my father's side of the
family, but on my mother's side we knew a lot. We
Calhouns are descended from Vice President John C. Calhoun, who is known in American history for encouraging
states to secede from the Union, for his role in the Civil War,
and for his support of slavery. It took me a while to realize
that the rest of the world didn't see history in quite the way
my family did. For example, I was taught that only very ignorant and uneducated people ever referred to the "Civil War."
That was an oxymoron because John C. Calhoun and our
people had already seceded from the Union; it could not be a
civil war because there were two separate nations. It should be
called, by people of education and distinction, the War
Between the States or the War of Northern Aggression.

Later, as a student, I came to resent our family heritage. I was not proud of being descended from someone who was a standard bearer for slavery, and therefore on the wrong side of a great moral issue in our history. Unlike the generations before me, I was not raised in the South. I did not eagerly claim my branch on the Calhoun family tree.

Perhaps because of that, my mother worked doubly hard to get me to see the contributions our family had made. She talked about the value of knowing one's roots and appreciating one's heritage, but I was not interested. So when I was twelve, she decided to organize a once-in-a-lifetime trip to Scotland for a large group of extended family members to trace our roots in the Calhoun clan.

Around that time Alex Haley's book *Roots* was capturing the world's attention. The story begins with the author's trip to Africa to trace his ancestors, some of whom were slaves. Referring to our planned trip, my mother explained, "Why, darling, it's just like *Roots*!"

"Oh, it's exactly like *Roots*," I replied. "Except we're tracing our roots back to the people who owned the slaves, who were on the wrong side of history, and who are already covered in all the history books. But other than that, Ma, it's *exactly* like *Roots*." I can feel my eyes rolling as I remember my words.

So a van filled with sarcastic teenagers, aunts, and uncles from South Carolina made its way from the airport in London to a remote town in Scotland. Despite my jaded attitude, I naively assumed that if we came all this way, family would be waiting for us. They'd invite us into the manor house and serve us dinner—or at least tea and shortbread. But the palatial manor house was also a museum, and we were asked to pay an entrance fee just like everyone else. Apparently Scotland is full of people related to the Calhoun clan.

We saw the gravestones of our relatives and traced them and the dates (back to the 1600s). Even a sulking preteen felt the connection to another world and to short, fragile lives. My mother had done a considerable amount of research. After finding our tartan she had us search guidebooks for references to the clan. She discovered that our clan motto was something that sounds like "conocolation," which translates to "gather up on the hill." So whenever our group was gathering anywhere, my mother would call out, "Conocolation!" and that became our tourists' rallying cry.

We asked a local about the word. He told us that our clan was known for "conocolation" because ours was the most cowardly clan in Scotland. Not only that, he said, but the Calhouns were scoundrels who made their profit unethically. Apparently our clan's prosperity came from forging letters with the names of other clans on them, and thereby goading them to fight with each other in the valleys. Our rallying cry was "Gather up on the hill!" so that we could hide while they battled, then swoop down and grab the spoils.

My mother was very disappointed in this but had us continue to comb through guidebooks. Finally I found a paragraph that said that one of our relatives had been a member of Parliament. "Now that's what I'm talking about," my mother shrieked happily. "Tell us what it says!"

"Mama," I asked as I read the entry, "what does 'expelled for sexual indiscretion' mean?"

My mother lit a cigarette. "Give me that %$*!@ guidebook."

When I recall this story, I remember that we are all immigrants, no matter how long our families have been in this country. We were all once strangers. Many African Americans were forced into immigration by slavery. Native Americans had their own migration patterns. Others came on the *Mayflower*, or in a truck, or by walking through the desert, but all were immigrants at some point. The founders of my own Congregational tradition came from England in search of religious freedom. They were American immigrants back in a time when there was no such thing as a "legal" or "illegal" immigrant.

But now things are much more complex. The issue of immigration is confusing and baffling to us as a society. It affects people in all parts of America, from our cities to our rural communities to the Midwestern suburbs where I live.

One of the most controversial issues is the question of undocumented immigrants. Fired up about that, we often forget that most immigrants—about three quarters of them—are here entirely legally with visas, or on the path to citizenship. The one quarter who are undocumented total about twelve million, although it's a hotly debated number and difficult to prove.

Of that twelve million, five million are children who are undocumented. Of course, if an undocumented immigrant has a child in the United States, that child is a citizen. So there are millions of documented children connected to undocumented family members.

This places a burden on social services and on our already convoluted and confusing health care system. Often undocumented workers are paying taxes because they're using a fake Social Security number. But although they're paying Social Security and paying into Medicare, they will never see or benefit from the investment. Many request a tax ID number because they *want* to pay into the system.

The American economy depends upon these workers. This dirty little secret does not get talked about very much, but most of us know people who work in industries that would collapse if it were not for the undocumented workers. They play an integral role in the American economy, whether we admit it or not.

Add to the complexity the issue of children. Children are born here and have citizenship, but if their parents are undocumented, their parents can be deported and the families broken up. When a mother is deported, she faces a horrible decision. Does she take the child with her, or does she allow her child to stay in the United States and be raised by others? A mother in this situation may come back into the country again and again, risking everything in order to be with the child that she wants to raise in a better life.

Children who are not born in the United States but are raised here have no part in the decision making. They grow up in this country and get to the point where they want to go to college, and they can't get any financial aid. They're stuck in low-wage jobs and unable to make it to the next level through education. In my neck of the woods, there have been more and more news reports of children raised in Chicago being deported and sent to Mexico with no memory of their home country. They are as out of place there as any foreigner would be.

There are a lot of loaded terms that come up in the debate. Some people call undocumented workers "illegals," taking an adjective and making it into a noun. In human history, when we take an adjective and turn it into a noun to describe people, it's usually a way of dehumanizing them, of saying they're not really people by taking the people word out of it. Most people who care about these issues prefer the term "undocumented worker" because it's more respectful of the humanity that we all share and draws attention to the work they do.

One of the dilemmas is how to protect the native-born worker from unfair competition in this uneven playing field. There is no question that an undocumented worker will accept substandard working conditions and a much lower wage.

Another dilemma is the so-called solution of the "guest worker," which seems to create even more problems. The guest worker is given a visa to come into the country like a migrant worker, who comes and then leaves. The guest worker's visa is attached to working in a particular place. But what if his employer is an unethical employer? What if it's an abusive workplace? He cannot easily leave the abusive workplace because his visa is tied to that job. This leads to the creation of substandard positions. Few people blow the whistle on a bad situation because the worker doesn't have full protection under the labor laws. But if we didn't have guest workers willing to work in these substandard conditions, might these jobs become full-time jobs with benefits and a union?

The path to citizenship is a problem too. Often people say, "I have nothing against immigrants, I just want them to come into the country legally." I challenge those people to research what it takes for a Mexican to enter the United States legally and gain citizenship. It's almost impossible, even if you do everything right and win the lottery system.

On top of this there is the issue of highly-skilled human capital. The immigration debate affects our prosperity as a nation and our ability to keep jobs in our country. It's not just that low-wage jobs are going overseas; high-end jobs are disappearing too. Many Americans work for companies that are moving their research and design departments overseas because the company needs U.S. visas for engineers in China and can't get them.

Finally, let's not assume that immigrants who clean the bathrooms in hotels, drive cabs, and mow lawns began their careers in low-skilled jobs. Many come here with college and graduate school education, with experience in engineering or medicine. But here they are considered unskilled. Yet they believe they can do better here than they could in their profession at home.

Unlike migrants, who move in order to find work on a temporary basis and plan to move again, these immigrants want to move to a new country on a permanent basis, in order to make an entirely new life.

On Sunday morning we read texts that are thousands of years old, sacred stories that trace the history of the Israelite people in and out of exile, and we remember how fluid those Old Testament national borders were. We might also remember that in the arc of history, much of the United States— Nevada, California, Utah, Colorado, Arizona, New Mexico, Texas—was once a part of Mexico. Like the Old Testament borders, U.S. borders have always been relatively fluid in terms of commerce.

But Americans tend to take a very short view of history. We react to what has happened most recently as though it has always been so and always will be. Our reactivity led to the immigrant backlash after the terrorist attack on the World Trade Center and the Pentagon in 2001. In our pain as a nation, and in our terror that this might happen again, we slipped into a level of comfort with racial and ethnic profiling that we would not have tolerated before that incident. Suddenly it became okay with us if someone who looked Arab was pulled aside for extra questioning at the airport. We allowed that state of terror to render our core values sloppy. Fear can do that.

Isaiah wrote, "Woe to the legislators of infamous laws, to those who issue tyrannical decrees, who refuse justice to the unfortunate and cheat the poor among my people of their rights, who make widows their prey, and rob the orphan." Woe to the legislators of infamous laws.

People will often say that America is a nation of laws, and that we have to respect the laws that we have in place or everything will unravel. They apply this principle to immigration, saying that there is no excuse to break the law and enter the country illegally. Inherent in that point of view is the unstated assumption that our immigration laws are just and worth following—that our immigration policies are fair and worthy of that respect.

But if you look at our history of immigration as a nation, it gives a much-needed perspective on our behavior in the past and on what the American people accepted as fair and just. Take, for example, the Indian Removal Act of 1830, which resulted in the Trail of Tears in 1838 and 1839, with seventy thousand Native Americans uprooted from their homes and their land at gunpoint. Consider the Fugitive Slave Act of 1850. If you helped a slave, you were violating a law that the majority of Americans accepted as just and fair.

The Page Law of 1875 prohibited Asian women from immigrating to the United States, supposedly to keep out prostitution. But the economy was riding on the backs of male Chinese workers, who were building the railroad for very low wages. Our government didn't want these men to settle here, form families, and put down roots, so they kept the women out.

Then in 1942 came Executive Order 9066, which gave the U.S. Army the power to arrest every Japanese American on the West Coast. In that time period, 120,000 men, women, and children of Japanese descent were sent to internment camps in isolated regions and kept under armed guard in one of the saddest stories in American history.

All of this, of course, was legal. In Arizona, a place that is near and dear to many of the snowbirds in my Midwestern congregation, they passed a law so that immigrants can be arrested without a warrant if they appear to be undocumented. How can a person "appear to be undocumented"? In the debates about this law, proponents suggested that one could recognize them "by their shoes." There's really only one way: by the color of their skin. The law's obvious racial profiling raises tremendous ethical issues for people of faith.

With twelve million undocumented immigrants, five million of those children, and a law that says we are supposed to turn one another in—are we asking our children to turn in their parents? Although laws like this will wreak havoc in countless families, many states are proposing them. I wonder what our record is on these and similar laws, and how history will judge us. What would Isaiah say to us?

We might ask ourselves if our own ancestors were any different from the immigrants crossing the border today. Although my mother's side of the family got all kinds of attention, we paid little attention to the Daniel side. My father's family had a low-key history of migrant farmers eking out a living, eventually buying a mule, slowly making their way to the middle class. So no one was more surprised than I when a church member did my genealogy for me and discovered that a member of the Daniel family came over on the *Mayflower*.

I was thrilled to get this news, not because I wanted the

pedigree, but out of a spirit of petty competition with my husband. He has long known that he is related to Captain William Bradford of the *Mayflower*, and has mentioned this to us many times. So I was breathless as I told him, "I'm related to someone on the *Mayflower* too! His name is John Howland, he was born in 1599, and he was a cabin boy."

To which he responded, "Well, that would be the last time anyone in my family got to tell anyone in your family what to do."

William Bradford is quoted as having called John Howland "a lusty young man." As a cabin boy or a servant boy, he was essentially a young man with no encumbrances, no family along for the ride, no nothing. He had agreed to come over and to sign his life away as a servant until the age of twenty-five. Only then would he get his shot at the American Dream.

I eagerly read the last will and testament of John Howland and his wife, to see what became of them. They were evidence that the Puritans lived almost as long as we do now, often into their seventies—despite drinking beer for breakfast. John, now a landowner, wrote his will and testament in his own hand. I was struck by his priorities:

> Know all men, to whom these presents shall come, that I, John Howland...will and bequeath my body to the dust and my soul to God that gave it, in hopes of a joyful resurrection unto glory. And as concerning my temporal estate, I dispose thereof as following...

He goes on to list what he's going to do with his fields and his property, almost as an afterthought to his more pressing spiritual concerns, and ends by saying:

> I will and bequeath my dear and loving wife, Elizabeth Howland, the use and benefit of my now dwelling house in Rocky Nook, in the township of Plymouth aforesaid with the outhousing land...I wish her to enjoy and make use of and improve of that land for her own benefit and comfort.

Clearly, he had come a long way since being a young, single immigrant on the *Mayflower*.

In her will, Elizabeth wrote, "It is my will and charge to all my children that they all walk in the fear of the Lord and in love and peace toward each other, that they endeavor the true performance of this, my last will and testament."

Elizabeth and John Howland wanted exactly the same things that we want. They wanted the same things that every immigrant today wants in that first generation: to own land and prosper on it, to see their children and their children's children thrive. They knew that they were loved by a God who does not see national boundaries, but who would judge them according to their kindness and mercy.

In my church the American flag stands below the cross, as does the denominational flag—reminders that one day, when we meet our maker, we will be rewarded, not for how well we patrolled our borders, nationally or theologically, but for how gracefully we crossed the divides that separate one group of human beings from another. In Christ there is no Greek or Jew, nor male or female, nor slave or free.

Ultimately we will not be judged for how well we followed the changing and sometimes unjust laws of a temporary nation-state, or for how well we patrolled borders that from the perspective of eternity will seem fluid and moveable. Instead, we will be judged on how well we followed the teachings of Jesus: "For I was hungry and you gave me food; I was thirsty and you gave me drink; I was a stranger and you made me welcome... in so far as you did this to one of the least of these brothers of mine, you did it to me."

I believe that the human spirit that compelled a young Englishman to sign up for duty as a cabin boy and cross the ocean for a better life in 1630 is the same spirit that compels a college graduate from Mexico to work as a hotel housekeeper, cleaning toilets and making beds, in order to send money back to her family.

That mighty human spirit is a gift from God that is distributed equally and without partiality in the hearts of all God's children. It will always triumph, ultimately, over cruelty and division, as long as we who believe in it stand up for our brothers and our sisters, for their dreams and for their families. Let freedom ring.

Part V

WONDERING

Chapter 22

Borne in Perplexity

I N THE DAYS BEFORE CHRISTMAS we hear in church about Mary's extraordinary dialogue with an angel, which ends with these thoughts from a young unmarried woman who was six months pregnant: "She was much perplexed by his words and pondered what sort of greeting this might be." I am sure she was perplexed.

Young Mary is restrained in how she describes her emotional state and in what she commits to. Having offered herself up in service to the Lord, having said, "Let it be with me according to your word," she does not go on to say this: "Oh, yes. And now I understand everything!"

No, the Gospel does not ever downplay the fact that Mary is perplexed, and that Christ's conception is downright confusing, even to his mother. Why, Mary is perplexed even before the angel tells her that she is pregnant.

As one who spends much of my life in such a state, I take comfort. I see this passage as a great anthem, a symphony, in honor of those of us who move forward not in clarity, not in certainty, not in single-mindedness, but with perplexity.

We're the ones at the back of the orchestra, hoping but doubting we're in the right place, playing with gusto nonetheless.

But we live in a society that favors decisiveness over perplexity. You are supposed to know what you want and act on it. There's no room for uncertainty. It's considered wishy-washy.

To which I would like to offer this gentle correction: If the mother of God got to be perplexed, you can be, too.

In fact, let's take perplexity out of the old broom closet, dust it off, shine it up, and put it out on the mantelpiece in the middle of the ecclesiological living room, because a little perplexity can be a wonderful thing in the life of faith. It's the people who ask the questions who get the answers.

Jesus, both born and borne in perplexity, can use my uncertainty and perplexity in service to the creativity and mystery of the divine.

Chapter 23

Inconsistent on Jesus

T HERE IS A GREAT *New Yorker* cartoon that has a clergy-
man standing at a crossroads where he is clearly
struggling with which signpost to follow. One has an arrow
and points to "Heaven." The other has an arrow that points
to "Discussion about Heaven." And he is clearly anguished .
about which to choose.

Sometimes, I think we in the church stand at the same
crossroads, stuck between "Jesus" and "Discussion about Jesus." This is particularly true of thoughtful, intelligent people
who are not afraid to ask questions about the Bible and the
history and culture of Jesus' day. We are so comfortable that
we are better at articulating what we do not believe about Jesus intellectually than saying what we do believe about him
personally.

But also stuck are the people who claim to know exactly who Jesus is, and then use that as a test to see if everyone else is saved or unsaved. I used to get really anxious around these intense people when they asked me, "Do you know Jesus? Are you saved?" I knew they had a particular definition of being saved that was not my definition. I felt I had to explain that and then add that indeed I was saved, if by that you could include salvation for good people of other religions, and that then they would look at me like I was either crazy or doomed. We've all had these conversations, and some of them have garnered us a free magazine. But now, when asked about salvation, I just say, "Yes," and leave it at that. I'm choosing the arrow that puts me on the path toward Jesus, rather than taking the road to the discussion about him.

"Jesus has been victorious!" yelled out a televangelist. "Jesus means you have the victory. You can be victorious."

"Tell that to the mother whose child is suffering from malnutrition," I say back to the television screen. "Tell that to the person whose livelihood has been destroyed by oil spills, expecting that God will clean it all up in eternity."

Alone, watching people on television whom I disagree with, I am always extremely articulate. You will have to trust me on this.

"Jesus wants you to be prosperous!" the preacher tells us. "The money is there for you, he just wants you to find it."

"Oh no, he doesn't," I explain back to the televangelist, pointing the TV remote at him like a lightsaber of truth. I do this with such moral and physical force that my small dog is temporarily unbalanced on my lap. Lucky, the pinheaded rat terrier, looks up at me confused. Why am I getting so worked up?

Since the televangelist is clearly not listening to me, I take the dog as my theological student and point the remote of truth at him. "Now, Lucky," I explain, "you and I both know Jesus didn't want us to invest in material things. That's just not who Jesus was."

At which point Lucky looks up at me as if to say, "So who exactly is Jesus?" pulling me out of the intellectual past and into the personal present tense, as dogs will do.

Now, when people tell you that their dogs look at them "as if to say," it means they are psychic, unbalanced, or better off lecturing their pet in theology than teaching your small children. But doesn't your dog ever look at you "as if to say" some deep question that is already on your mind? If not, you probably don't think that televangelist could hear me either.

So who am I talking to in those conversations, if not my dog or the people on television? Who are any of us talking to when we rant in our heads in passionate debate? In my mind, I am talking to Jesus, who sits beside me in the family room or in the next seat over on the bumpy airplane or rides shotgun with me in a traffic jam and particularly delights in me when I listen to talk radio. It's Jesus, my constant companion, who knows me exactly as I am.

But there's another Jesus I also believe in, one whom I would not wave the television remote at, but would fall prostrate before in the presence of his unimaginable beauty. This is the resurrected Christ, the Lord of all things in heaven and on earth, the one who inspires the music, architecture, and art that make us shiver with recognition that we have, through such things, brushed up against the divine.

This is the Jesus I want to let Paul describe. "He is the image of the invisible God, the firstborn of all creation; for in him all things in heaven and on earth were created, things visible and invisible, whether thrones or dominions or rulers or powers—all things have been created through him and for him." Here, Jesus the Christ is bigger than time and space. All things were created through him. He preceded his human self. This is not someone you yell at while listening to talk radio, but one who inspires you to be silent, humble, and awestruck.

We can have endless debates about who Jesus is. Is he the risen Christ who made my forgiveness possible through his blood on the cross? The one who exists outside time and space and was there at the creation of the universe? Is he the spiritual teacher who lived a human life from which we can gain wisdom and courage?

The debate sounds to me like being presented with an amazing banquet and then being told to pick only one adjective to describe it. So one person says it was salty and another says it was sweet, and they argue as to who is right.

But if you know anything about the human tongue, it was created to have spots that pick up on sweet and salty, and even sour. Tastes are complex, beautifully so. Sometimes you react to one flavor more strongly than another. You taste different things in the same dish. But none of that affects the dish itself. Its taste changes in everyone's mouth.

Is it wishy-washy to perceive Jesus in many different ways? To experience him at one moment as your best friend and another moment as the mysterious peace that passes all human understanding? To picture him reigning on the throne of heaven triumphant over evil at the day of reckoning? Or to picture him screaming out in anger at God from the cross? Which one of these gets it right?

I don't want to choose. The church has plenty of tents staked out on the battlegrounds of who Jesus is, and why it matters. I pitch my tent in the field of mystery, and have yet to nail it down.

In a life-changing moment when I was twenty-one years old, fearing for my father's life, alone and weeping in the chapel at the hospital, it was Jesus the personal savior who put his hands on my shoulders and asked me to surrender to him completely. I did, and felt a lightness I had never felt before in my life, a light I still carry with me.

And it is Christ the King on the throne of heaven who came to my heart when I saw the glaciers in Montana. The view from the mountains seemed to be from another universe, so stunning and strange I wanted to sink to the ground and avert my eyes. Or was that carsickness?

And it is the Jesus who said he wanted to gather us up like a hen gathers her chicks who accompanies me on the heart-wrenching work of parenting, who gathers me up from the crumpled heap of failure that every parent has known, and that only a mothering savior can see.

And it was because Jesus gathered so many sinning misfits together at the table that I can picture myself belonging there too. And it's that same welcoming Jesus that makes me long to share a table with Jews, Muslims, and Buddhists as a foretaste of a heavenly banquet where there will be room for us all.

And it is in the teachings and sayings of Jesus that I find myself so directly spoken to that I cannot imagine finding a spiritual home where he was not the absolute center of it all.

When it comes to Jesus, I am inconsistent. But I come by it naturally.

The same God who created human beings to be idiosyncratic and inconsistent decided to come to earth in that same idiosyncratic and inconsistent human form. It's like God was trying to get a ten-pound sausage into a five-pound bag. No wonder we are confused as to what we have been served.

We human beings tried nailing down Jesus, on the cross, and he refused to cooperate. Instead of dying, he rose from the dead.

And now, he is seated at the right hand of the Father, right next to me and my dog, Lucky, on the family room couch where, from the throne of heaven, he wields the remote, hears our intimate complaints, takes out the splinters from the wounded hands of the world, and somehow rules the cosmos that he created in the first place.

Talk about inconsistent. Thank God for it.

Chapter 24

Quibbling and Quoting

S O WHAT DOES YOUR church believe?" If someone asked you that question, what would you say? In the spirit of confession, let's acknowledge that many of us in progressive, open-minded churches might respond by telling the person what our church does *not* believe.

We might say, "We're not closed-minded, but open to all ideas. We welcome everybody, unlike some other churches. We're not like the fundamentalists who take scripture literally. And we're not like the churches who won't ordain women."

"Okay," says the patient inquirer. "So what *do* you believe?" We might continue, "Well, we believe that people can be free to believe many different things, so that's a tricky question to answer."

"Okay, then," says the inquirer, now less patient. "Then what do *you* believe?"

"Well, I'm on a journey. It's a private matter. Here are the authors who have meant something to me and can say it so much better than I could... Blah, blah, blah."

Oh, just stop it.

We are told that one of the things that impressed Jesus' listeners was that he spoke plainly, not quibbling and quoting like the religious scholars. He just put his beliefs and teachings out there and was ready to withstand some debate.

You can be open-minded and still know what you think. You can be accepting of other people's ideas but still willing to articulate your own. You can rejoice in the many diverse paths to God and still invite your neighbor to church. Just say it.

Chapter 25

I Don't Have to Prove It

I CAN'T PROVE TO YOU that Jesus lived, died, and was resurrected, nor that he healed people on the Sabbath or that he forgave his tormentors. I can't prove to you that one God can also be three in one, and that together that force has parted the waters, burned bushes, and fed thousands on short rations. None of this can I prove. But I can tell you that I have faith in it.

I can say it because "faith is the assurance of things hoped for, the conviction of things unseen." I can hope and believe in what is not before my eyes. I don't have to be logical, and most of all, I don't have to prove it. Not to you, not to anyone.

In our culture, it seems like people of faith are always on the witness stand being asked to prove things, and we Christians tend to cooperate. We come up with the search for the historical Jesus and scholars who vote on whether Jesus said this or that. Or archaeological studies that will finally prove whether or not Jesus was resurrected. Documentaries on the History Channel draw us in, as if finally we might look reasonable to the viewing public, as though finally we will get our proof.

I'm tired of playing by that dull and pedestrian set of rules, which has everything to do with a litigious, factoid-hungry culture and nothing to do with following Jesus. I don't come to church for evidence or for a closing argument. I come to experience the presence of God, to sense the mystery of things eternal, and to learn a way of life that makes no sense to those stuck sniffing around for proof.

Chapter 26

The Limits of Taste

I LIVE IN AN AFFLUENT, fast-paced suburb of Chicago that pretends to be a simple, slow-paced village circa 1950. We have a cute little old-fashioned movie theater. We have coffee shops and pizza joints the kids can walk to, beautiful parks at every turn. We have a baseball parade when the kids start their season, a homecoming parade for the teenagers, a puppy parade at the dog park, and a Fourth of July parade that takes over the entire town and turns the day into a twenty-four-hour party.

An African American tumbling troupe is always the highlight of the parade; they come in annually from the city, stopping at our town and many others in what must be an exhausting but lucrative fundraising day. Another highlight is the Republican Party float, with its enormous life-size paper mache elephant, usually accompanied by our own home-grown congressman, raised in the town that he returns to in triumph each Independence Day, usually waving from a convertible. The Democrats make a small showing, of course, but given that I seldom recognize any of them, I have come to wonder if, like the tumblers, they are also imported from elsewhere for the parade.

On ordinary weekdays, our children walk to school, accompanied by their mothers and a few fathers. The parents walk a few steps behind to make sure their children are not viciously attacked by other well-cared-for children.

People refer to the town as Mayberry, some with irony, others without. But just miles outside of America's third largest city, there is our little village, a small town, if you will. Our tree-lined streets, with children playing in the yards, take you back to a simpler time when most kids played pick-up ball in one another's yards and had bonfires on cool fall nights. We still do that.

In our town, we love our kids. So much so that we put signs up about them in our front yards. GO HITTERS, says the sign that indicates a high school football player lives within, and not a badly behaved toddler as I first suspected when I saw a sign advertising "hitting."

There seem to be signs for all the sports, but lest you think it's all about the jocks, you can put a sign in your yard indicating that your little one is in the marching band or even a member of an elite, internationally known children's chorus.

When I think of poor Jesus, showing up as a grown man

in his hometown to preach and getting such a poor response, I wonder how he would have fared in my own little village. Look at the flag-waving homecoming we give to our congressman each year. Look at the signs we put in our yards for our kids, the bumper stickers that reveal we are the proud parents of honor students, our children's colleges proudly displayed on the back windows of our cars. See how we love our hometown boys and girls. Surely Jesus would have fared better here.

But, of course, there is a great deal those signs in the yards do not say. Not every attribute of our youth gets mentioned. I have yet to see any yard signs that point to certain still popular extracurricular activities.

How about this sign? "MY KID SPENDS A LOT OF TIME IN THE BASEMENT."

Or these: "TV WATCHER," "VIDEO GAME EXPERT," "DOES NOT EVER CLEAN HER ROOM," "SLACKER."

How about these signs? "BACK TALKER." "FIGHTS WITH SIBLINGS." "REGULAR AT DETENTION." "MY KID WILL SELL HIS ADHD MEDICATION TO YOUR KID."

Oh, come on, it's not fair to describe our kids that way. That's not who they are, really, deeply and underneath. But why display the other attributes then?

What if we tried to get a little more honest and revealing with the signs, a little more nuanced and real? We'd need smaller print of course, or bigger signs to say something like, "My daughter is a member of the dance team, which I hope will pull her out of a clique of shallow, underachieving gossipers who I am convinced have brought her grades down, but

169

sometimes I wonder if their parents think she's the problem." That would be a yard sign worth pulling over to read.

Or what if we just said, "Inside this house lives a complicated kid with multiple interests whose life is far too fragile and complex to be described by his membership in any one group. But if you really want to know more, his résumé is posted on the family website."

Or what if the signs were about the whole family? "DIVORCE UNDER WAY." "MEDICAL DEBTS." "WE COULDN'T AGREE ON A PAINT COLOR SO WE PICKED ONE WE ALL HATE."

Visitors to our town always comment on the signs, but not just the signs about the kids. You see signs that adults put up too.

Yes, we have our political signs, but while there are a few of those, that's hardly unusual. No, the ones that visitors notice are the issue signs. As soon as residents disagree with one another over a given issue, signs go up.

In that way we are much less like a small town and much more like a busy, fast-paced suburb. No to this and yes to that. It's a shorthand debate. What it lacks in complexity it gains in certainty. Yes to this. No to that. The sign has been posted.

There used to be far fewer ways to express one's opinions than there are today. Once you know your opinion on an issue, there's a sign for your yard. You don't have to make it yourself; someone is waiting to supply you with one. Now, post it on Facebook, send it out on Twitter, and put it on your blog. It's my opinion, I believe it, it happened to me or to my kids, it is worthy to be shared. And I determine that myself. You're almost under an obligation to tell people what you think.

Why don't you have a sign in your yard? Why can't we tell which activities your kids participate in? Why aren't you posting on Facebook?

Well, couldn't we just...talk to one another about these things?

Why can't I respond to an e-mailed party invitation without being asked for my favorite movies to share with all the other guests?

We are quick to ask one another to share information, but equally quick to judge. Because in this tweeting, texting world where every opinion can be shared, every child's activities advertised, with photographs sent from a cell phone to the Internet, and every angry thought e-mailed anonymously with the press of a button, this exchange of information can be quick, but sometimes it can cut deep.

We are creating a culture of narcissists who have never had a thought they did not press "send" on.

I think it, I felt it, I did it, and now it must be shared. Once shared it becomes real.

And now you must respond. Did you see my post? This is the bargain we have struck, instantly available to one another electronically but unavailable in person, our teenagers checking e-mails and posts under the dining room table because they have seen their parents do it.

Can you believe the number of people who tell the world what they're eating or drinking? *While* they are eating and drinking. "Hey guys, I love this new restaurant." And I'm thinking: Well, just eat then.

People who worship their own opinions will at some point have to come face-to-face with an idol that like all idols will disappoint. If I worship my own opinions then I will delight in you sharing yours until they differ from mine, and then we are into the sign wars. Because if I feel it, it must be true.

Sentimental, happy thoughts and angry, outraged-citizen thoughts seem to get equal airtime these days, and we can switch from one to another with great speed.

Oh, look at darling Jesus, he has grown up so handsome and articulate, and here he is preaching to us in the temple he attended as a child. Look at how far he has come. Listen to how clever he is. Let's give him a spot in the big parade.

Interesting how the Gospel of Mark, in its baffling brevity, in its refusal to fill in all the plot details, does not tell us a word about what Jesus said. All we know is that suddenly, the hometown hero ticked people off.

Yes to this or no to that. And then the small-town crowd got suddenly nasty.

Well, he's only a simple man's son, not from a particularly educated family. There were very few signs in Mary and Joseph's yard when Jesus was growing up. Mark says, "He's just a carpenter—Mary's boy. We've known him since he was a kid. We know his brothers, James, Justus, Jude, and Simon, and his sisters. Who does he think he is?" And the scripture says, "They tripped over what little they knew about him and fell, sprawling. And they never got any further."

Riding by in our cars, insulated from one another, protected from conversation or the revelation of real life pain, we read the signs in the yard, about who is for this, and who is against that, whose child plays in the orchestra and who does nothing, and I think we are like those villagers. We trip over what little we know about one another and we never get any further. Trapped in the world where our opinions have come to matter so much, they weigh us down in incivility and relativity.

In this "it's all about you" culture, worship is profoundly countercultural. Worship is directed toward God. If there's anyone I want to get something out of worship, it's the creator of all things seen and unseen.

Someone was complaining to me about why she had stopped going to her church, saying, "You know, when I was sitting there in worship I just didn't get much out of it."

To which I replied, "Well, it wasn't directed toward you."

"I'll go to worship," said one person about another church, "but only if it's the contemporary service. That's the only kind of music I like."

But what does it mean when our worship services are segregated and advertised as being spaces where you will hear only music soothing to your ear?

If there's anyone I want to take delight in a beautiful anthem, it's the one who invented musical taste in the first place. It's not all about us and our taste.

Which is why I love it that we do not segregate ourselves at my church based on musical taste. You never know what you will hear on a given Sunday. That's because music in worship is not for us, but for us to offer to God, the expression of a wonderful variety of styles.

And it's the same with preaching. If there's a target audience for a sermon it's probably the guy who died on the cross for preaching his own.

When Jesus Christ himself showed up to preach, in the very town where he was raised, a celebrity who had healed people of their diseases and drew crowds wherever he went, the townspeople were at first excited, but in the human condition of drowning in our own opinions, it went very quickly awry. For, while technology has changed and complicated things, I think the human condition is pretty consistent. The limits of taste are sin.

For even then, when faced with a word from the Son of God himself, it was still a matter of opinion. And they essentially said, "You know, I just didn't get much out of that. I'm taking my Jesus lawn sign down and replacing it with something else. I'm defriending him on Facebook.

"But don't take offense. It's only my opinion."

In the church at its best, we challenge this idolatry of opinion and acknowledge the limits of our own taste. We acknowledge that the love of God matters more than our love of the latest fad. And we tap into a long tradition, a historic tradition, that takes the best and the wisest of thousands of years of following Christ and, while the world is asking you for your favorite movie or your latest opinion, we say prayers and make proclamations that have been shaped by the lives of others who came before.

In church at its best we are a vagabond group of naysayers saying no, it is not all about you, in this moment.

The customer is not always right. When Jesus preached in his own town, the people said, "I didn't get much out of that."

And two thousand years later we read about the limits of their good taste.

But it's so tempting in this competitive culture of super-achieving children whose accomplishments are advertised, as obviously as their parents' accomplishments are advertised in the size of their house or the make of their car or the degrees they've earned, so tempting to think that we have to get it right.

So tempting for me as the minister of a church in the middle of all that to want to get it all right. We're struggling with this together.

It's tempting to get caught up in the idolatry of our tastes and opinions and to think it is all up to us.

At my previous church in New Haven, the building was beautiful but faded in its glory. The paint peeled on the high ceilings, the magnificent organ needed repairing, and parlors were filled with disheveled antiques and velvet couches with one broken leg, next to a beanbag chair.

The lovely old chapel that had once been the site of charming small weddings and elegant tiny funerals had the old wooden pews ripped out and was now an all-purpose room with blue vinyl-covered chairs. The pastor before me was proud to have turned the chapel into something useful, where twelve-step groups could really use it.

But I longed for the beauty of the whole place to be restored. I couldn't preside over an entire capital campaign or bring the whole place back to its former glory, but I could work on that little chapel. It would be my legacy. We researched old photographs and had a carpenter re-create those beautiful old pews and restore the little chapel to a wedding-worthy setting with rose pink walls, and the AA group decided to move to the room downstairs, where they could put chairs in a circle. All was well, and more beautiful besides.

Many years after I left that church, I began to have a recurring fantasy about what might happen next. The next pastor would pull off a big renovation and with great eagerness I would accept his offer of a tour of the building. The huge sanctuary would glisten with new paint, the basement would be transformed, and the place would be perfect. With each new room, I will gasp at the wonderful transformation that had taken place.

"But this is one of the changes I am most pleased with," the new pastor will say. And as my fantasy continues, he will then fling open the doors of the little chapel. "That space was quite unusable and we needed more space for children's worship, more of an all-purpose room, but we had a devil of a job pulling out all those old antiquated pews." And there in the middle of my beautiful chapel will be those twelve blue vinyl chairs arranged in a circle. "Today we call it an all-purpose room. Much more what we need in this day and age, don't you think?"

One day in eternity, I imagine all the characters in this fantasy are going to stand in front of the throne of Jesus waiting for judgment and it is then that he will tell us which one of us was right about the chapel. Two votes for the all-purpose room, and one for the chapel. Oh please, Lord, let it be me. Can I at least make my case?

And Jesus will look down and call us forward one by one.

To the first, he will say, "You were right to care about the recovery of addicts and to open that space up for those life-saving meetings."

To me, he will say, "Lillian, you were right to care about beauty and worship, and to expect that even the smallest funeral deserved a dignified setting."

And to my dreamed-up successor, he will say, "You were right to follow the movement of the Spirit to allow the children a space to worship.

"But as for those blue vinyl chairs, I didn't get much out of that.

"Pews, vinyl chairs, get over yourselves. You are here for eternity, people. So here are the keys to your eternal homes all next door to one another on clergy row, behind the next cloud. Move in and go ahead and put big signs in your clergy yards that say, 'Jesus says I was right.'"

And then it's going to hit me, and I may be brave enough to ask him out loud, "Wait a second, you mean to tell me that heaven is a place where all the clergy of the same church live next door to one another in the same clergy subdivision with self-righteous signs in their yards?"

And Jesus will respond, "Oh wait, Lillian, this is really awkward." There will be a long pause and then a sigh. "So you thought this was heaven?"

No, in heaven nobody has a sign in their yard and nobody cares about vinyl chairs or wooden pews and nobody gets to say, "You know, I didn't get much out of that."

Because to be in the presence and power of God, at the heavenly banquet, in the presence of an inimitable host, we will finally know the limits of our taste.

Part VI

REMEMBERING AND RETURNING

Chapter 27

Every Spiritual Home

THESE DAYS, VERY FEW PEOPLE who join our church were raised in the denomination or tradition we are a part of, and we are hardly unique in that. Most of my church members were raised in other forms of Christianity that were less open-minded than ours, and they may have some negative feelings about the church of their childhood. And so they drifted from church and sought to go it alone, without a faith community.

But eventually, they hit something that was bigger than private, self-created spirituality. Perhaps it was the death of a parent, the birth of a child, a friend's illness, or a lonely patch in life, but suddenly they found themselves remembering some of those childhood Bible lessons. They found themselves recalling the blessings of the Christian faith, and they searched for a church, but they did so very tentatively, not knowing what they would find and afraid of being hurt.

When they do find us, they have the same reaction that so many people do when they discover a welcoming and inclusive church where you are not expected to leave your brain outside on the sidewalk. "This is the church I always wanted to find but didn't know existed." But our church isn't perfect any more than the churches they left are all bad.

A miraculous thing can happen to grown-ups on a faith journey. We come to appreciate moments from our past faith community, as different as it may be from our current one. We may recall a special Sunday school teacher who taught us the "sacred writings" in our childhood.

That is why when people join our church, we always say, "We give thanks for every community that has ever been your spiritual home."

I believe that there really is a connection between who we were raised to be and who we are now. It might not be a straight line, but you can connect the dots. God works through all kinds of religious communities at different points in our lives.

No spiritual home is all good or all bad. So give thanks for the small and tender blessings of every place that has ever been your spiritual home, and for lessons you have learned.

Chapter 28

The Secret Passage

I N THE MINUTES BEFORE the wedding ceremony, I wait downstairs in Pilgrim Hall with the groom and the groomsmen. Upstairs, the sanctuary is lovely, with freshly vacuumed carpeting and wedding flowers that are a cut above the usual Sunday morning carnation extravaganza. But down where I wait with the men, it is the usual ugly church fellowship hall, with its folding metal chairs, chipped Formica tables, and years of cookie crumbs and juice ground into the rug.

"We used to run around this place like crazy," the groom tells me, as other young grooms have told me before, recalling their upbringing in the church in which now they will make their wedding vows. "We'd stay down here with our sleeping bags for youth fellowship lock-ins. But we'd run around all night, sliding on the rails, playing games. We never slept."

It is an irony for these young men raised in the church that in the minutes before their elegant weddings, they will wait downstairs in Pilgrim Hall where, over the years, they sprinkled glitter on glue-dripping felt banners, ate chicken casserole, drowned their Yule logs in showers of spray-on snow, and played dodgeball late into the night.

These grooms always reminisce, saying, "We used to run wild here," as if confessing a secret that as pastor, I would not know. Yet still today, the old church hall reflects, in its shabbiness, a wide variety of activities of a holy space well used. It is a shelter for the homeless on Sunday nights, a banquet hall for a Hawaiian dinner in a snowy season. It is an indoor playground whose handicapped ramp seems to have been constructed so that packs of children could run down the slope and swing their little legs and then their whole bodies over the rail like gymnasts.

"Kids, get off that thing!" the youth fellowship leader says. "You cannot run wild in here!" But of course they can, and they do, as they always have.

The groom pulls the best man aside to explain, "Sometimes, we just took off exploring into this creepy old secret passageway that ran behind the back of the church." His look is wistful, as he tries to convey to his buddy, to me, and perhaps to himself, that he has not always been tuxedo-clad husband material, about to make promises for an adult lifetime. He was once a raggedy, rebellious teen, tearing around the church, searching for secret hideaways amid the exotic mysteries of growing up. Perhaps he has cuddled with a girl in this place. After all, there's a reason teenagers agree to get locked in the church all night.

"You may not know about that secret passage," he tells me, as the minister. "Has anyone ever shown it to you?"

"We're going to use it right now," I say. "It gets us from Pilgrim Hall to the door that opens out to the front of the church."

And so he joins those grooms who have taken the long walk into the sanctuary to be married, through a short, dark passage in which he once played chase, Sardines, and perhaps even stole a kiss.

We walk up some old stairs, and then into the passageway, which takes us past the back of the organ, around some Christmas pageant scenery and a broken music stand, and there, we wait at the end of the passage, behind a thick wooden door. A peephole, a little curved glass eyeball, allows us to peer out at the faces of the people in the pews, to check to see if the doors behind them have yet been thrown open to reveal a flower girl, a bridesmaid, or even a bride.

The groom notices that the view through the peephole is distorted, so that straight angles are curved, familiar faces are blurry, and the world outside that door looks like a twisted wonderland. But it is as clear a view of the future as any of us can hope to get. We all see through a glass darkly.

So often the wedding scripture comes from Paul's first letter to the Corinthians, the famous chapter thirteen. These are the words that strike couples as fresh and ministers as overdone; words about love being patient, kind, and everything but blind. The clergy must explain that these words were not written for couples, or for romance, but were delivered to the larger body of Christ.

Still, during the wedding, everyone hears, "Love does not insist on its own way," and notes it as another piece of good advice for newlyweds, up there with "Never go to bed angry" and "Don't forget to say 'I love you,' every day." Couples seize upon 1 Corinthians 13 as a rare practical word from that relentlessly impractical book. "We like this reading," the couples tell me. "It's good advice. It makes sense."

But marriage makes so little sense. The actions that take place at the front of the sanctuary will be as mysterious as the travels through the secret passageways of youth fellowship. Amid the clanging cymbals and gongs of any marriage, love jumps out unearned, illogical, and miraculous. In marriage, we promise to love when it makes no sense, as Christ has loved us when it made no sense.

The groom sees his mother seated. Now he thinks he observes a flash of white at the back of the church, the fluffing of a dress he will see for the first time in just a minute; a hint that the woman he plans to spend his life with is hidden, but there waiting, as he waits. He presses his hands against the passageway door, leans forward, pasting his eyeball up to the peephole, as close to his future as he can get from here. "For now we see through a glass darkly, but then we will see face to face."

"The youth fellowship, the overnight lock-ins...Do you guys still have those?" he asks me pensively. "Do the kids still run wild and do crazy things all over the church?"

"They sure do," I say. "But this may be the craziest thing you've done here yet."

The groom steps back from the door. He breathes in and stands up straight. Adjusting the flower in his lapel one last time, he pulls open the old door and prepares to meet his bride.

With one foot in the old secret passageway, and another stepping out into the church, he freezes, as if something has just occurred to him. His great adventures are not behind him, but out in front.

Chapter 29

Valentine's Day

T HERE ARE ALL KINDS of theories about how we got Valentine's Day. People agree that the original Saint Valentine was an early church martyr, but which one was he? I found three possible candidates from the early centuries of the church, but all we really know is that it was established as a day to honor the saint by Pope Gelasius I in A.D. 496. But how did a feast day associated with a martyr come to be associated with love and romance?

One theory relates to the ancient Roman festival of Lupercalia, which was observed February 13 through 15. Lupercalia was an archaic rite connected to fertility. Apparently, Pope Gelasius I (492–496), the same guy who established Valentine's Day, abolished Lupercalia. But given their proximity of date, perhaps St. Valentine, a Christian martyr who had nothing to do with romance, got morphed into the mascot of a fertility rite. And you know what wild fertility rites lead to. Dancing. And flowers, chocolate, sweet notes, and a nice dinner out. And then maybe you get the fertility rite.

Well, the religious origins of Saint Valentine's Day are so sketchy that it was eliminated from the Roman Catholic Church's calendar of saints back in 1969. But certain myths about that martyr have sprung up around the holiday none- theless. One myth holds that the martyr, whoever he was, was jailed not just for being a Christian, but for standing up to the Roman emperor Claudius II, who had declared in a law that all young men had to remain single. Apparently he did this in order to grow his army. Because if you can't express yourself in one way and, shall we say, "exercise your creative passions," you might as well go off to war and be really, really angry at your enemies.

But this Christian Valentine went against the emperor and performed secret marriages, hence that love connection, and that's what got Valentine thrown in jail. The legend got ex- tended to include a story in which Valentine fell in love with the jailor's daughter, and just before his execution, he wrote her a love letter that he signed "Your Valentine," thus being the first Valentine and establishing the tradition of the Valen- tine card. Isn't that neat? Unfortunately, none of it appears to be true.

The first documented love connection between Valentine's Day and the church was the work of the poet Geoffrey

Chaucer, who, in his 1382 poem "The Parlement of Foules," wrote this line:

> *For this was on seynt Volantynys day*
> *Whan euery bryd comyth there to chese his make.*

How we got from birds hooking up to people hooking up on Valentine's Day, historians are still debating, but for now, the love connection is there. So, if you've ever wondered if the holiday is just a made-up day for the greeting card industry to make some money, rest assured. The nonsense surrounding the holiday goes back way further than that. You cannot return to a pure Valentine's Day because it has always been a muddle of a holiday with highly suspect origins.

Typically assumed to be a day when lovers exchange heart-shaped boxes of chocolates, roses, and romantic cards (or, depending on how long you've been married, fast food while driving someone to band practice), on February 14 our hearts turn to our hearts, and to those who make our hearts beat, with all kinds of interesting cultural manifestations.

For some parents of young children, the holiday can be all about the kids, as you spend hours the night before generating twenty-five cards for twenty-five elementary children who do not yet know how to read, but still all expect to receive a Valentine from everyone else in the class.

For people who are dating, Valentine's Day can be an awkward time, with multiple potholes of potential misunderstandings. "Okay, thanks so much for that really extravagant piece of jewelry, but given that we've gone on only two dates, I didn't even get you a card." Do you call? Do you make a fuss? Do you not?

It can also be a time of stress for long-term couples. "Okay, I thought *you* made the reservations..."

"But you told me not to get you anything this year!"

"Yeah, but I didn't mean it!"

Or it can be a time of low-key domestic joy, when children make cards for their parents, or grandparents send something in the mail, or like when I got home from a long day of work Monday night to see that my husband, Lou, had made steaks and a great meal all around, which we ate with my seventeen-year-old son, who by the same time next year would not be around the house on Valentine's Day. So Lou's steaks and that three-person Valentine's meal at the kitchen counter beat out any fancy restaurant, to my way of thinking.

But whatever your stage in life, or your beliefs about the holiday, we traditionally use this time of year to tell the people we love that we love them, from friends to children, to family, to lovers, even pets. Yes, if you can believe it, there are Valentine's cards for pets.

Okay, can I vent for a minute? Who buys a greeting card for a pet? Now, we all think our pets, just like our kids, are of above average intelligence. But honestly, here's a news flash: your dog cannot read.

And for the person who really overestimates his pet's intelligence, in this fast-paced electronic age, you can actually send an e-mail card to your pet. Really? Well, that's a good

191

use of everyone's time. I picture the scenario of the e-mailed pet cards in my own house.

"Bruno, are you on the computer again? Get off and let Lucky have a turn. Honestly, it's a beautiful day outside and you dogs have spent the whole day on the computer.

"Now, put on your leash, and that little doggie suit I got you, because we're going out for our Valentine's dinner. And let's put you in this Seeing Eye dog disguise so you can get into the restaurant.

"I know it's dishonest but I really want us to have this special time together. Unless you tell me I am underestimating you, Bruno... You're giving me that blank stare again, Bruno, like you have no idea what I'm talking about.

"Bruno, did you forget to make the dinner reservations? Just like last year, I go out of my way to make Valentine's Day special for you and you do nothing!"

The truth is, love is complicated and sometimes love hurts. An old Gaelic blessing sums it up well:

> May those who love us, love us. And those who don't turn
> their hearts; and for those who don't turn their hearts,
> may they turn their ankles, so we'll know them by their
> limping.

But in the end, we don't want that. We want love, and lives filled with love. We don't want arguing and discord and to know our enemies by their limping. We want harmony and kindness and love. But love takes its knocks. In a fast-paced world of Internet dating, texting, and sexting, love seems easier than ever to come by. But it's just as complex as it ever was. And when our lives move as fast as they do, with cell phones, voice mails, hyperscheduling, and overwork, love suffers.

At the point when people are too busy to sit down and eat together, and others are e-mailing cards to their pets, you know we are living in a fast-paced world where love has to fight to get any room.

But that rich and romantic book of scripture, the Song of Songs, reminds me that sometimes you have to say to the people you treasure, "Rise up, my loved one, and come away." Come away and stop all you are doing, and give yourself to love.

Sometimes we rush through life so fast that we don't make time for love. We take it for granted. One spouse mutes the television during a commercial break and says, "Hey... We okay?"

We look at our college-age kids heading off to school and realize there just wasn't enough time during the break to tell them how treasured they are. A relative we haven't spoken to for too long suddenly passes away and we realize there were so many conversations we should have had, if only we had picked up the phone. Why didn't we stop to say, "Rise up, my love, my fair one, and come away, and spend some time with me"?

That is one reason that Valentine's Day creates such pressure on us. The whole country goes hearts-and-flowers nuts, with expensive dinners, pressures on dating couples, and cards for pets and children who can't read them. We overdo it because, secretly as a culture, we know we're not really that good at love.

In an explosion of hearts and flowers, we can distract ourselves from the slow reduction of lukewarm relationships that sit on the stove of life, unstirred, unseasoned, and increasingly tasteless. Those can be marriages, friendships, and family relationships—all of them needing more time than we have given them. Who needs to hear from you, "Rise up my love, my fair one, and come away, and spend some time with me"?

We all make these plans. We say we'll take the fabulous trip, the cruise, or the hike through the mountains, and then we'll have that time. But somehow that trip gets too extravagant to happen now. The trip in the future becomes the placeholder for all the hard work of relating, day to day, until love has left the room and no one wants to go on the trip anymore.

"Rise up, my love, my fair one, and come away, and spend some time with me," doesn't have to be a trip to Paris. It could be a trip to the $6.99 Indian lunch buffet next to the grocery store.

It doesn't have to be the hyped-up trip to Disney World where, under the therapeutic leadership of Mickey Mouse, finally the entire family is going to get along. It could be a trip to a basketball game.

It doesn't have to be the perfect mother-daughter shopping trip in the city, but it could be the long-needed mother-daughter bedroom cleaning adventure, where together you hunt for four-month-old Doritos under a bed that has never been made. "Come away, my love, my fair one, and spend time with me. For love is stronger than death."

Because as lovely as it is to steal away somewhere beautiful and quiet and safe with a loved one, for so many of us, that's just not how life is. Love can't wait for the perfect sunset, or the quiet beach, or the ideal moment when we have all the time in the world. For most of us, love is in the here and now, and we shouldn't wait for Valentine's Day to honor it.

Love is right here, where we live, at church, at your kitchen table with old friends, in your scrapbook memories, in your hopes for college, in the retirement party, in the cards sent, and in the pictures saved. Love is right here, every day, with or without chocolates, flowers, and dinner reservations. Love is right here.

But has your life been moving so fast you missed it?

One day the water heater in my basement sprung a leak, and I prepared myself to write a big check. What I did not prepare myself for was to be awash in memories.

Water had filled a large plastic container of photographs from my parents' home. As the repairman installed a new water heater, I carefully pulled out wet photographs from those old, sticky albums and dried them out on the kitchen counter. Suddenly, on a night when I was way too busy for this trip down memory lane, a broken water heater had forced me to stop what I was doing, and suddenly, I was awash in memories from my childhood and teenage years.

I found pictures of my first cat, followed by pictures of her first batch of kittens, followed by pictures of her second and third batches of kittens. Eventually, I found a picture of a bunch of cats gnawing on a turkey right out of the Thanksgiving serving dish on our old kitchen counter. The inmates were clearly in charge.

My teenage daughter and her friends were snacking at my kitchen counter as I dried out the old photos. I was happy to provide the comedy for their evening. I just wish the source of it hadn't been my mullet haircuts and home permanents.

There were old school essays, report cards, and chatty letters to my parents, now both deceased. In one note I wrote as a fourteen-year-old from church camp, I asked them to mail me a picture of my prom date. I suppose I was in need of evidence that I had one.

And, of course, there was my first published essay, from an airline magazine that had had a contest. I would love to know how I came to enter it, but the ones who must have encouraged me to do that are now long gone from this world.

That water heater broke just days before my son's eighteenth birthday. When he is my age, will he think that the faded crinkled images of his childhood are worth saving, and worth fighting for?

Like me, he will probably find some evidence that his childhood was not perfect. For instance, I had to ask myself, when confronted with the photographic evidence: Did my parents really celebrate my confirmation day with a cocktail party? No wonder I wanted to be a minister.

As a child, I always fantasized about some perfect trip to Disneyland, where we would all be happy and be the perfect, normal family.

We never went to Disneyland. But surrounded by all those pictures, in a messy kitchen turned upside down, looking at my fourteen-year-old self, I saw that love was there.

As a child, I wanted to take any images of my family's imperfection and wipe them clean.

But as an adult, I want to wipe them off in order to preserve them—just as they are.

Because love was there.

Chapter 30

A Grade of Incomplete

L ITTLE CHILDREN IN SCHOOL are taught the importance of completing their assignments. In college, if you don't write your final paper, you get a grade of "incomplete," which seems to imply that when you finally write that paper, you will be complete.

But then we become grown-ups, and we discover that most of our important jobs are never complete. We may finish up one aspect of a project at work, but that leads to another one. A student may complete a homework assignment, but the teacher has a job that is never complete. Many of us have jobs that are never complete.

Take parenting. Parents of small children will look at the parents of teenagers and say, "Tell me it gets easier!" But parents of teenagers will tell you that it just gets more complicated. Parents of adult children tell me that the job of parenting is really never done. Kids move out, and then in many cases, they move back in. But even if they live in their own place, it's not as if our children ever graduate from needing parents.

You don't one day suddenly complete the job of parenting. It continues even after your children have children, and are doing that job themselves, with those same incomplete results. In life, we don't get a gold star for getting the big jobs done. Rather, I think God gives us a gold star for hanging in there, still working, in the incompleteness of life.

For in the end, people are not complete until God completes us. One day, we will meet the alpha and the omega, the beginning and the end. We will see God face-to-face, and finally be complete. But until then... there's nothing wrong with taking the occasional incomplete.

Chapter 31

Little Boots

A CONTAINER OF Kentucky Fried Chicken appeared to be dancing in the middle of the dark street, with a life of its own, so my husband and I stopped to investigate.

Out of the chicken box crawled a terribly skinny kitten with long black fur and four bright white paws. She had been making that box dance, as she tried to lick out the last crumb for nourishment. Now she purred, leaning into me with her whole body. We adopted that little stray and named her Little Boots.

Little Boots thrived with cat food, a trip to the vet, and lots of love. But she remained very small and displayed the silliest behavior. She would sneak up on our other cats, as if to attack them, but she would be right in front of them, in plain sight. By the time she pounced, the cats had moved away. She couldn't figure out how they knew she was coming.

It was only when we found her walking on a second-story porch rail, precariously sticking her paw out into the air to feel for her next step, that we realized the obvious. Little Boots was blind.

From then on, that cat became my hero. Nothing stopped her. When she ran into a wall, she turned back and ran the other way. When she walked into a piece of furniture, she remembered where it was the next time. She didn't sit still. Her little white paws were always out in the air in front of her, testing, to find her next foothold.

She was tiny and the world was dangerous. But Little Boots seemed to walk by faith, not sight. She was the perfect companion to take to divinity school.

We moved that little cat to four different apartments in New Haven, and each time she had to relearn the lay of the land. Each time she had to adjust.

I found myself having to adjust when, in my last year at Yale Divinity School, pregnant with my first child, we learned that Little Boots had a critical medical condition. As a grad student living on loans, saving for a new baby, we had no money for her expensive treatments, treatments that had no guarantee of working.

Seven months pregnant, I became so despondent that I couldn't eat. I stopped bathing and changing my clothes. Eight months pregnant, hormones swirling my moods like a bad cocktail, I lost all energy except for the energy to examine my rotten life and to ask the hard questions. How would I take care of a baby when I couldn't even provide for my cat?

How was I to choose between savings and a blind little crea-ture who had moved around the country with me? Where was God? In the end, all the questions had the same answer: I was in no position to bring a new life into the world.

Now, I had faced greater tragedies in life than the loss of a cat. So there was a part of me that observed myself falling into melancholy with enormous judgment. And, of course, that didn't help. I could add "self-indulgent and self-pitying" to my list of problems.

Sunk into melancholy for days, I would watch Little Boots sleep on my pregnant belly, rising and falling with my breath. The cat was unaware of her condition but was clearly slip-ping away into more and more hours of sleep. Given that I was not fit for the job of pet owner, and was also going to be a terrible mother, it was all I could do to get myself to class, since it had become crystal clear to me that I would be a ter-rible minister as well. But I got out of the house and made it to school, where I was pretty sure nobody would want to sit next to me since I certainly did not want to sit next to myself.

"We've taken up a collection," Marie said as she pushed a thick envelope of money into my hand after chapel services, with a stern look at my dirty clothes. It was like the envelope drug dealers share on television, slipped to me furtively, and when I opened it, I could immediately see that it contained hundreds of dollars. "It's for Little Boots," she whispered. "Now you can take her to the vet."

I barely knew Marie. She was a middle-aged biologist who

wore small wire-rimmed glasses and sensible sweaters. She taught at Yale Medical School but for some reason had decided in her fifties to study divinity. She had always struck me as logical, scientific, intelligent, and not particularly emotional. Yet it was she who had taken up the collection. Was she just one of those passionate animal lovers? Or was she a passionate people lover? I never got to ask her, but rushed back to give my husband the news that Little Boots had been rescued once again. We went to the vet with the envelope full of anonymous donations.

It turns out the treatments did not work. After a lifetime of low-hassle moves, Little Boots slipped away to her next destination serenely in my husband's arms, and without resistance. But as sad as we were, we were left serene as well. We were not haunted by the thought that we could have done more. We had done what we could, not because of our own power but because of a community that decided to pitch in, and the Holy Spirit that runs through it. I had wondered where God was, and God had shown up.

In the aftermath of the cat's death, I was able to turn my attention back to preparing for motherhood. I regained my appetite, and fortunately for my husband, my desire to bathe. While what lay ahead of me seemed at times impossible, now I knew I wouldn't have to do it all by myself. I was not going to be alone in the next big adventure.

I found myself thinking often of Little Boots, my role model for the easygoing traveler. She was always ready to adjust to her surroundings. That blind kitten traveled light and was open to anything. Her long cat stretches were nothing compared to her inner flexibility.

And, of course, she did not overexamine her life. In that, she had the benefit of being a cat. But she also seemed to be a particular kind of cat, the rare kind that expects the world to be a loving and delightful place. Unable to see the pitfalls or her potential attackers, she stuck her little paw out ahead of her to feel her way. While she never could see what was ahead, she seemed to trust that she was surrounded by love. And, of course, she was.

When I think of all the creatures I have loved and lost, I am struck by one thing. I thought I was taking care of them, but really they were taking care of me. And I think this is exactly what God had in mind. We're here to look out for one another.

Eighteen years later, that baby I was carrying is heading off to college. In some ways I feel as helpless to protect him as I did back then. But what I know now, after eighteen years of parenting, is that his welfare was never up to me alone. There has always been a cloud of witnesses, a community to step in and make this hostile and lonely world a loving place worth exploring.

So eighteen years later, as I prepare to see my son leave this house and go out into the world, as I watch him stick out his paw to see what's next, I remember Little Boots, who walked by faith and not by sight.

Chapter 32

Trial Separation

WHEN I WAS TEN, my parents sat me down in our formal living room to explain that my dad would be moving out for a while. "Are you getting a divorce?" I asked.

"No," they said. "This is just a trial separation."

My ten-year-old emotional barometer had gauged the tension between them. My young ears had heard the arguments. My still-growing heart had learned to beat to the rhythm of their occasional anger. The night before, my father had hurled a glass at my mother across the dinner table, and I had hidden in my bedroom as they fought and shouted throughout the night.

Perhaps a separation might be worth trying. At least it meant our family was trying something.

I worried I would never see my dad, but I ended up seeing

him more than ever. He took me to the new James Bond movie, and then out to a restaurant to eat spaghetti. We had one-on-one conversations we had never had before. For a few months our little family tried the trial separation and I confess that I liked it.

And then I felt guilty for liking it. Everyone had told me that divorce was devastating, and what child wants to see their parents divorce? I certainly didn't.

But in reality, I welcomed the reprieve from all the tension in the house. I was ready for a break from the fighting. Both parents seemed sad, but also more relaxed apart from the other. When people asked me if I was upset about my parents' situation, I said that I was, because I knew that was what I was supposed to say. But there was a big part of me that liked it. And for that I felt guilty.

I've since learned that I am hardly the first child to feel that way. Often parents dread breaking the news of a separation to their children only to discover that the children had been hoping for some sort of action all along. Sometimes with the pain of separation there is also the relief of pain.

And then just as suddenly, the deep conversations and spaghetti dinners with my father stopped. There was a sudden change of course that felt to me like so much of my childhood life, as though the course had been set by a navigation system far away from the cheap passenger seats. I knew the direction had changed when I came home to our apartment to hear the tinkle of ice cubes being dropped into cocktail glasses, as my parents laughed and flirted on the balcony. They had always had sparks with each other. Those sparks could be like a trigger on a bomb or the kind of sparks that begin a cozy fire that warms a room. These were the latter kind of sparks, the cozy ones. And suddenly I knew that my parents were getting back together, as I eavesdropped on them from the living room. When they came in from the balcony, they seemed giddy, a bit boozy, and hopeful. "Your daddy is moving back in," my mother giggled. "Darling, isn't that wonderful?"

I wasn't so sure. At the age of ten, I was already a cynic. At the time, a popular song was "All You Need Is Love," but I knew you actually needed more.

Soon, the old dynamics swept over our family once again like an irresistible wave, pulling us into the riptide of rusty resentments and sorry score keeping. I retreated to my room on many evenings.

The trial separation may have come to an end, but now, living together in the same house, we were trying out separation all over again.

This is a truth that is not often shared: you don't have to live in separate places to be separated. There is much play-acting in the world, and often on the stage of suburban streets or chic urban condos, where from the outside the family looks like a unit, inside there is a rift that cannot yet be exposed to the light of day. So we make assumptions that this family is happy and complete, and that one is broken and in pain, but really we have no idea. We ought to treat every family with tenderness and compassion for the all the things we do not know about them, and pray that they will deal gently with us too.

Separation can be physical but spiritual too. Looking back, our family was always moving in and out of trial separations, whether we lived together or not.

Years later, when they finally got to come out of the closet, if you will, not as gay but simply as two people who could finally admit that they could not live together, there was pain and resentment, but a miraculous thing happened over time. They seemed to be able to connect with each other, more not less, as their lives grew apart. Ironically, it was long after my parents had separated for good that I felt we were most connected as a family.

By the time I was an adult, I didn't have to worry about how they would get along at my wedding. And when the time came to say my own wedding vows, it occurred to me that my parents were still trying to keep theirs, long after the marriage had ended. Living apart, they could still love and cherish each other. They could still support each other through sickness and in health.

They got to the point where they would include each other, with their new partners, in holiday gatherings so that everyone could enjoy the grandchildren. Don't get me wrong, we couldn't have all stayed yearlong in such close proximity, and there was a reason I never lived in the same state as my parents as an adult. But those times of trial connection remain for me precious memories of what life could be, and perhaps will be like in heaven.

I once was talking with someone toward the end of his life, and with his last breaths in his hospital bed, he growled, with as much force as his dying body could muster, "Do not call my brother! We don't speak. I don't want him involved in any decisions."

I knew that these two siblings had always been at odds with each other, but with the pain of illness, as death grew closer, the bitterness between them grew as well. I wished it could be different. I had hoped that as one brother grew closer to death, they might grow closer to each other. I had hoped that they might reconcile, but instead the animosity grew more intense.

There would be no Hallmark card moment for these two brothers, no tender deathbed reconciliation. After years of going to bed angry, the dying man was now going to his deathbed angry.

I didn't judge the anger. I had heard the reasons for it, and I would be angry too. But I still grieved the estrangement and hostility. I wished it could be different.

When earthly reconciliation cannot happen, or does not happen, I remember Paul's words from his letter to the Romans: "For I am convinced that neither death nor life, neither angels nor demons, neither the present nor the future, nor any powers, neither height nor depth, nor anything else in all creation, will be able to separate us from the love of God that is in Christ Jesus our Lord." Since eternity exists outside of space and time, all of humanity may well experience that moment together, regardless of when or where we die. All trial separations will come to an end.

*   *   *

We human beings are always trying out separation, but I think that God is consistently practicing connection. Remembering that about God makes me look at my life with grander ambitions, and makes me want to try out connections in the here and now.

Could your most caustic relationships be redeemed?

Is there a trial separation you might want to end?

Is there someone you cannot reconcile with by your own power, but you might be able to by the power of divine grace and mercy?

In many ways, I think that's why people come to church. Out there in the world, they tell you everything has to be fair, and when it's not, you can get revenge. In church you hear about Christ dying on the cross next to sinners so that we might all finally believe that there is nothing, absolutely nothing, that can separate us from the love of God.

And if that's true, then what is to keep us separated from one another?

I look back on what happened with my parents and I want to be careful not to make them sound too sweet and perfect. My father never stopped driving my mother crazy with his stubbornness and she never ceased to irritate him with her dramatic ways.

I know there were tensions for them both as single parents that were like an iceberg, of which I saw only the tiny tip. But when I think of how that iceberg seemed to thaw over time, how seasons of resentments seemed to melt away like water flowing into the ocean of life, I consider each drop of water, each tiny hurt, that slid into the sea to be a tiny miracle. It's a miracle I am not sure would have been possible for them were it not for their faith and the teachings of the Christian church.

My father had never been an enthusiastic churchgoer when he was married, and it was my mother who took us into the Episcopal Church. My father was raised in the Disciples of Christ, in Tennessee, a church that baptized believers in a great tank of water, a church where every special event was celebrated by potlucks of countless casserole dishes lined up in the old church hall, a carousel of comfort food where Jell-O and condensed soup were the key ingredients. But as a married couple, my mother had chosen a very different church for them, the more formal Episcopal Church, which my father attended sporadically and without great enthusiasm, a church he referred to as "smells and bells."

So it was a surprise to me in high school, when shortly after my parents finally separated for good, my father attended and then officially joined an Episcopal church in downtown Washington, D.C. The church was within walking distance of the new efficiency apartment he had furnished with one card table, one folding chair, a single bed, a television, and a Doonesbury poster still wrapped in plastic that leaned against the wall on the floor. His spare and depressing single man's apartment was a dramatic contrast to the cavernous, dark, Gothic church with its gold leaf paint and extravagant stained

211

glass. And I was surprised that after all that talk of smells and bells, his new church was known for its high and formal liturgy, as well as its serious work with the homeless.

Most Sundays, there was one man who would stride into the service right in the middle of the prayers, wearing a dramatic floor-length black velvet cape and wildly colored bell-bottom pants decades after anyone was wearing such a thing—this was the Reagan-era eighties after all—but in he would come with his platform shoes and enormous sunglasses. "I'm here," he would announce in the middle of the quietest prayer time in the worship service, as he strode up and down the aisle. "God is here! Here I am, folks. You can get up off your knees now. It's me—I'm God. Relax, people, I really don't require all that."

And the liturgy would quietly continue to rumble under his ramblings until he found a seat, occasionally up front with the clergy, if there was a spare thronelike seat up there. There he would sit and preside for perhaps a minute or two, and give the occasional royal wave to his mumbling people, and perhaps exclaim once again, "Get up off your knees. I told you, I don't need all that." And the steady service would continue, as solid as the grace and mercy of God among feuding and broken people.

When my father told me that there was a nice lady from the congregation he had befriended at a church supper, I pictured an elderly woman he was taking groceries to or driving to the hospital, as some kind of a mission project. When I finally met this beautiful and vibrant woman who shared not only his passion for writing but his love of their common little church, I figured out they were dating. It was at such a church in a denomination that his former wife had dragged him into that my father met the woman who would eventually become his life partner, someone who seemed to be the person he was always meant to find. At that little church, having once been lost, it seemed that now he was found.

And at my mother's new church in the city, she found the lively friends and fellow adventurers who would accompany her on her journey into newly single life.

I loved attending worship at my mother's extravagant church, where red wine was sold at a cash bar at all the catered church suppers and champagne was served at Easter communion. On one famous Sunday the avant-garde priests rode into the sanctuary on motorcycles, and to this day I can't remember the theological reason, because after seeing something like that, who would?

But I also loved my mother's new church because it was in its basement that my father discovered his favorite Alcoholics Anonymous meeting, and made another profound and life-saving connection.

I attended an AA meeting with him one evening, and an elderly homeless man with taped-up glasses who reeked of urine and sleeping on the streets, approached me and asked me where I went to school. When I told him I was a sophomore at Bryn Mawr College, his face brightened, and he said, "Why, my wife went to Bryn Mawr! We met when I was a student at Princeton." Then the man, who I had assumed I had nothing in common with, went on to describe all the prettiest landmarks of my college, as well as all the traditions we still kept up to that day. The man who seemed to have nothing in common with me had once shared the same college experiences that were shaping me that day. It was humbling. Somewhere he had a former wife who had never predicted she was marrying a man who would spend his later years alone and on the street. But there in the holy space of a church basement, our lives seemed more connected than separated.

Looking back on that strange night, at my father's AA meeting in the basement of his former wife's church, I realize that we human beings spend our lives in a trial separation from one another. We think we have these divisions, disagreements, past grievances, divorces, class differences, and separate paths in life, and to us they feel profoundly real.

But in the meantime, the Holy Spirit keeps knitting us back together, miraculously often through the church, reminding us that nothing can separate us from the love of God. Not even one another.

Many years later, my mother became ill and I watched my father keep his marriage vow to love both in sickness and in health. He was no longer her husband, and there were others to stand at her bedside, but he too kept vigil from a distance.

It is a strange kind of pain to watch someone die who once you loved as you loved no other, and now your place and role are different, but still you grieve, and I know he did. Nothing can separate us from the love of God, not powers nor principalities, not legal papers nor old scars and family feuds. For my mother, the trial separation of human life was ending, and the connection with God was unfolding, as all of us were drawn into the beautiful pain of knowing what is precious and what is not.

And it was at my mother's funeral service that my father finally moved upstairs in her beautiful church building, and for the first time took a pew in the transcendent worship space above his favorite church basement, where before he had rested upon an old folding chair. Now he joined the other mourners on the faded velvet cushions of old pews well worn with prayers, some of whom had watched him marry the woman we now said good-bye to. Now he joined the friends and the family, and by now he was both.

We all turned to the pastor to hear a word of comfort at the loss of one who had died far too young. As the old hymn promises, "Oh love that will not let me go, I rest my weary soul in you." We were there to hear the promise of God that one day all of our trial separations will end.

And it was there that I heard my mother's voice, calling out to me from the past, as if noting that finally the three of us were all at church together, father, mother, and child, the whole family, finally all at church together.

"Darling, your daddy is moving back in. Isn't it wonderful?"

And in a strange way, it finally was.